The Right Rock is a sincere yet playful devotional filled with wit, wisdom, and vulnerable stories. This book invites young adults to journey with Jesus and, like Josh does in his daily life, he vows to go with you for 100 days.

Brandon Bennick, *The Center for Faith and Leadership*

In *The Right Rock*, Josh Rothenberg shares daily words of wisdom and encouragement that help remind the reader that they are not alone in their journey with Jesus. Drawing from his personal experiences, scripture passages, and stories, and appropriate cultural references, Josh's reflections are whimsical and weighty at the same time. There is a sincerity in his vulnerability and a kindness to his words that makes him a great companion for any young, or young-at-heart, follower of Jesus.

Welford Orrock, *Kairos Initiative Coordinator,*
Baptist General Association of Virginia

THE RIGHT ROCK

100 DAY DEVOTIONAL

JOSHUA ROTHENBERG

The Right Rock: 100 Day Devotional ©2025 by Joshua Rothenberg

Published by hope*books
2217 Matthews Township Pkwy
Suite D302
Matthews, NC 28105
www.hopebooks.com

hope*books is a division of hope*media

Printed in the United States of America

First paperback edition.
Paperback ISBN: 979-8-89185-235-8
Hardcover ISBN: 979-8-89185-236-5
Ebook ISBN: 979-8-89185-237-2
Library of Congress Number: 2025939828

Dedicated to the Center for Faith and Leadership.
It's now hard to imagine doing life without y'all.

ACKNOWLEDGEMENTS

First and foremost, I'd like to acknowledge that without the continual strength from the Father, *daily* intercession from the Son, and the active person of the Holy Spirit within me, none of this would have been possible.

Thanks to Brian Dixon, Hope Dover, and all the people from hope*writers who have made this effort manageable and doable and enjoyable. Special shoutout to Amanda Mc-Mullen and Glorida Day for guiding me through the bulk of the editing part of this whole process. I'm a better communicator and writer because of y'all.

Mom and Dad, thank you for my ultimate cheerleaders and best friends. Nick and Meg, you guys have been and always will be my heroes. Brandon and Rick, your friendship and steadfastness means more than you know. Reese, Jack, and Nora, you are the brightest lights in my life and being your uncle is one of my favorite things ever.

To the boyos I'm privileged to do life with, I'll keep beating a dead horse: you are my brothers, and I love you all dearly. Period. End of story. Goodbye. The end.

To the Disability Resource Center, much appreciation towards Seth, Janice, Willow, and Aric for giving me opportunities to lead others towards independence and teaching *me* a lot about independence in the process.

To my dear friends over Zoom, Aiden, Charlie, and John, you'll never know how much life you all give to me. I'm privileged to "do group" with you all.

To say nothing of the awesome ministries I get to be a part of: Chancellor Baptist Church, YoungLife Fredericksburg, and the Center for Faith and Leadership.

To the Chancellor staff, thank you for letting me be a part of a team whose mission is so clearly lived out. A big shout out to the young adult group that's been so consistently doing life together. A very, *very* big shoutout to Vic Meadows, whose genuine love, joy, and faithfulness have spurred me on my best and my worst days.

To my fellow YoungLife leaders, thanks for encouraging me to love relationally in ways where the Gospel can be seen in tangible ways. In particular, a big thanks to Randy, Anna, Hayley, Randall, and Bryan from Team Capernaum. I love getting to make Jesus famous with y'all in the goofiest and funnest ways possible.

To the Center for Faith and Leadership, for loving me exactly as I am, for seeing things in me that I don't always see in myself, for being my best friends and my family, thank you. Special shoutout to Emma, Sarah, and Brandon for the sacrifices they make so young adults can know where real life is found. That same shoutout also goes to their spouses Michael, Gordon, and Becca, whose sacrifices are just as meaningful and appreciated. *Another* shoutout to Kip Foster, for Mason Dixon and Panera breakfasts, authentic hospitality, and profound wisdom on Fridays at 11 a.m. that comes in the form of poignant and Spirit-filled one-liners.

TABLE OF CONTENTS

INTRODUCTION

Greetings, my most excellent friend. That's a *Bill and Ted* reference, but I'm getting off-topic.

My name is Josh Rothenberg. I'm a University of Mary Washington student pursuing a bachelor's in creative writing with a minor in disability studies. I have the privilege of being on the leadership team for YoungLife Capernaum, a disability-tailored ministry within YoungLife that exists to make God's love accessible to kids who often feel lonely or ignored. Some of my favorite hobbies include writing things from my own fantasy and superhero stories to theological ponderings to cheesy one-liners I keep in my notes on my phone; reading authors like C.S. Lewis, Bob Goff, and oldies-but-goodies like John Bunyan; working out—or "gains for God" if you will; singing my lungs out to the inspired words of esteemed artists such as Brandon Lake and Kermit the Frog; drawing original characters and redrawing when I update the lore of my story for the hundredth time; watching movies (especially Marvel) and TV with the people I love most; being "Uncle Josh" to the three best youngins in the world; listening to podcasts from Mike Winger and J. Vernon McGee (absolute GOAT teachers of the Bible); studying theology, church history, and apologetics, and learning from sources like J. Warner Wallace and

Sean McDowell (absolute GOAT apologists); and doing life with the greatest birth family in the world that I love more than they'll ever know and with the coolest family of choice that is the Center of Faith and Leadership here in Fredericksburg, Virginia.

My main source of joy, of course, stems from the Lord and His love for me, and as of late, I haven't found a better way of reminding myself of His love than having dedicated time to study His Word intently and continually seeking His face in prayer daily. Any spiritual growth plan you take that doesn't involve those two things in any meaningful and applicable capacity is doomed before it even begins. Whether you like it or not, college is a time when you leave and lose things you were taught. Some really hard things you carry with you into college could honestly stand to be lost. There are other things, though, that you should *never* lose. Three guesses as to what I'm referring to ...

Various studies estimate that between 60 and 80 percent of incoming freshmen who profess the Christian faith leave it by the time they graduate. This could be due to many factors, such as legitimate church hurt and lack of accountability in leadership, many unanswered questions or doubts about God or Christianity, and failure to see it lived out in front of them. Regardless of one's reason, I'm pretty confident that a lot of it has to do with the fact you go in feeling alone. I'll take feeling sad with a community that loves me to death over feeling sad by myself any day of the week. We can try to find a remedy for the cracks and look inward for the "fix," only to be surprised when they just get deeper and longer and wider. When that inevitably fails, we can go to relationships, grades, popularity, or even doing noble things as the basis for our worth and identity. Again, we'll still be surprised when those things eventually fail us. The hard truth is that the world can't give us the peace, hope, and meaning we seek because it's looking for it, too. If looking in and looking out doesn't work, the healthy alternative is to look up to God, as that's the only thing that can truly satisfy.

Just a little backstory: I have autism and OCD. I was raised in a Christian home, believing in God and Jesus, but not necessarily raised in the church, so the things I have to say about intentional community and life in the Body of Christ are still discoveries I make every day not knowing what that was like for many years. I hadn't thought too much about my disability until the beginning of middle school when forming friendships became much harder and less organic. Aside from a few exceptions, no one ever really excluded me. No one went out of their way to welcome me either, though. My logical mind made it hard for me to believe there was a Creator who existed. I eventually got answers in regard to His existence, but the internal storm still raged on for a good while. I realized the turmoil wasn't just doubt of His existence, but doubting that I was really a masterpiece, as He says we are (Ephesians 2:10), instead of a waste of matter and oxygen made from leftovers. Scraps. Not invisible. Not noteworthy. Something that just kind of exists. Those were the intrusive thoughts going through my head as being diagnosed with OCD from a much better place. My family was always there for me and still is, but I needed more connection than only with people who were my age. I needed a Friend closer than a brother (Proverbs 18:24), who accepted me for me (Psalm 139:13-14) while still calling me to new and better things (Mark 1:16). I'll be honest: loneliness and living with two disabilities were hard, but that wasn't the main issue. The issue was that I knew deep down doing life on my terms wasn't working and that following Jesus was what I needed, but I wasn't willing to let go of the hours of violent and penetrating things I was exposing my mind and heart to, along with my whole life (Mark 8:23). I don't know why I was shocked when my anxiety and intrusive thoughts got worse when I was passive about being intentional with what I put before my eyes and how long I did it. I was in a dark place and unwilling to go to the only place for help. Anyone else would've given up on me. Thankfully, God's far more stubborn than even I am and wasn't satisfied with me not hearing what He gave to make a relationship between us a joyous reality.

I was introduced to YoungLife my freshman year of high school. I wish I could say I finally met a ton of friends in high school and formed real connections. I wish I could say I no longer struggled with feelings of loneliness and I felt peace again. Due to a combination of struggling to connect with others and a fearfully and wonderfully made neurodivergence in a sinful and selfish person, things weren't really improving. I did end up giving my life to Christ at YoungLife Fall Weekend in 2019 and started to make more efforts to spend time in His Word and talk to Him. Things were improving, but not as fast as they could have had I let go of the things He was asking me to let go of such as seeking validation from others and trying to derive my meaning from the things of this world. Then Covid hit and changed everything. I'm not going to be insensitive and say 2020 was an amazing year. Overall, it *wasn't* for *many* reasons beyond the pandemic. It took a lot of things from me personally. What it did give me, though, was uninterrupted time in the morning to spend with Jesus. I'm not exaggerating: the first time I read His Word and prayed with the intent of seeking Him for its own sake rather than having to impress anyone, I felt all the persistent and restless anxiety I had felt for the past four and a half years vanish from me instantly. I felt peace for the first time in years. I felt loved beyond what I could even comprehend. I felt safe and secure and confident—I was tasting and seeing that the Lord is good. And—get this—I felt like myself. The truest version of me, not the me I was looking to the other things for. Once I truly got sold out to Jesus, everything in my life changed and all for the better. I started eating better and not just Vienna sausages (you can ask my dad for horror stories), I started writing my own stories instead of being a mindless consumer of someone else's, and the love I knew I was to have for others got easier as I was shown again and again in His Word of His love for me. I'm not advocating that feelings alone equals experiencing God—we shouldn't go to God just for an adrenaline high. I speak from experience that there are going to be days where, for some reason, you just don't feel like God is nearby. I'm going to tell you something I wish someone had told me when I was struggling with all of this: your feelings about God, others, and yourself are not facts. They're subjective, individual bodily responses to specific situations and, therefore, should not be treated like objective truths that dictate and govern how you live. God does the heavy lifting, but if He's only responsible for His part in this relationship, that logically means we're responsible for our part.

I still didn't have anyone besides my awesome Young-Life leader Andrew and family I was particularly close with, but, honestly, I still was content because I had my relationship with God. Nonetheless, I knew that the community I wanted and that God wanted for me (basically Hebrews 10:24-25) wasn't happening yet. I had grown to love my alone time with Jesus, but I still hated feeling alone. I had this fear that I would go through college being a hermit, not by choice, and be unable to make connections with folks who don't just love me but like me. I was hopeful that my last YoungLife leader in high school, current area director, and now good friend, Caleb Rittler, lived near campus. Still, I needed a community that would remind me of my first love with Abba. It's not an exaggeration to say I was 90% sure college would just be high school: alone but with more debt. I find it bonkers, bananas, and just plain crazy how God can take the minuscule 10% of faith you have in Him and do the craziest things. To make a long story short (It's a really good one you'll hear about), I opted to have a roommate and prayed he would be nice and have a reasonable sleep schedule. I didn't know he would become one of my favorite brothers in Christ and lifelong best friend. I decided to check out the ministry that made such an impact on my life. I didn't know I'd get to lead and love kids who are going through the exact things I went through. I stuck around even amidst the initial awkwardness of meeting new, like-minded folk. I didn't know they'd be my and my family's answered prayers for the people I know to love me and accept me as I am. I decided to try out for an internship at a church. I didn't know it would end up being my home church where I get to be loved on and love others into what God is calling them to be. I chose to read Jamie Winship's *Living Fearless* after settling into the awesome community that is the Center. I didn't know God would say very clearly to me that I'm a "dreamer" and would give me the idea to write this devotional.

I'm not trying to suggest that following God will always be sunny and peachy. Looking back, I was given opportunity after opportunity to know God and others more deeply even after taking my faith seriously but when such a thing as doing work-crew for YoungLife over the summer came up, I backed out of fear of losing my comfort. I missed chances to form deeper connections with God and the people who were trying to meet me where I was. God is good enough to make bridges for us to be with Him, and it is an awful shame if we don't at least take the first step across. I'm not saying I'm perfect at it, but nowadays, I try to give God the time of day to show me the challenge and joy of discipleship and see how that can change everything for my good and His glory. I invite you to consider the adventure God may be inviting you to follow Him on and even reconsider whether you're already on the adventure. College doesn't have to be the period where you protect your faith: it can be where it can thrive and have ripple effects for your and others' eternity. The changes God wants to make in your life and in the lives around you in this period through prayer, Scripture, and fellowship can be categorized as the "what" of living from the center. It's ultimately not about knowing the "what," though. The key to living from the right rock is knowing the "who."

DAY 1

FROM ADOPTION INTO IDENTITY

Ephesians 1:5

In *Kung Fu Panda 2*,[1] the protagonist Po grapples with the fact that he was adopted by Mr. Ping, a goose he assumed was his birth father. Tigress, Po's close friend in the movie, says it best; "That ... must have been quite a shock." His question of "Where did I come from?" quickly becomes "Who am I?" Lord Shen, the villain who orphaned Po, cruelly remarks that his parents didn't love him. Eventually, Po learns to move past his pain and find inner peace, which reaffirms his identity as Mr. Ping's son.

We are all, on some level, looking for peace with our past pain and ourselves—symptoms of not knowing our real identity. It wasn't always like this, of course, but ever since Adam, we have been scrambling to find a secure identity, something we once had in God. However, as we're remind-

---

1   *Kung Fu Panda* 2. Directed by Jennifer Yuh Nelson, performances by Jack Black, Angelina Jolie, and Gary Oldman, Paramount Pictures, 2011.

ed in today's scripture, Jesus planned for us to be adopted into His family again, giving His heart joy to do so. In a pivotal scene in the movie, Po has to redirect a cannonball fired at him by the peacock warlord to obtain his new identity. Thankfully, in Christ, the only thing we have to do is repent and ask for it.

Father,

Thank you for adopting us into Your family. May we step out in confidence and walk boldly because You have given us this brand-new identity.

In Jesus' Name, Amen.

OUR GOOD FATHER

Romans 8:15

The word "Abba" means "father" in Aramaic, and I had known that prior to going to college, but I had never once heard someone refer to God as that audibly in prayer before. That changed when one of my closest friends referred to God as "Abba" when she and our other friends were praying in a group. Calling God my Heavenly Father and believing that as a fact was daunting because as an autistic person, tangible and visible things are easier to wrap my mind around. I also didn't want to associate Him with the word "father" to avoid the thought of disappointing Him. That prayer session began a dramatic paradigm shift. I realized that what Paul was saying was that God is not a perpetually disappointed employer tolerating me, but my eternal daddy who loves me as much as any of His other sons or daughters. His discipline is just another form of His loving care. Let's follow my friend's example of approaching our Heavenly Father and praise Him for being a truly astounding one.

God,

Thank You for being such a wonderful "Abba." Grant us the grace to always see You as the One who brings us comfort, love, and protection as only a good Father can.

In Jesus' Name, Amen.

DAY 3

GOOD AL HOSPITALITY

1 Peter 4:9

My mom and so many others can attest that Al Hurt, my late Pop-Pop, would have given you the shirt off his back if you had asked him. He didn't have a whole lot, but that didn't stop him from treating every person who stepped into his home like family. My mom says he didn't know a single stranger. He loved hosting parties and sharing food and laughter with those fortunate enough to have known him. He wasn't perfect, of course, but that didn't change the fact that he was probably the kindest man I have ever known. I'm grateful for the time I had with him. Unfortunately, not everyone is as welcoming and genuine as my Pop-Pop. We can be overlooked by others or do the overlooking. It hurts to be seen as an afterthought or "in the way." I think everyone wants to be warm and welcoming but they fumble because they just don't know how or who to look to for inspiration. Fortunately for us, we serve a God who showed us the perfect example of generosity by giving us the perfect gift in His Son Jesus. So, the next time you see a coworker, classmate, or someone else by themselves, remember to give them some good old West Virginian hospitality and welcome them, knowing you've been welcomed into an everlasting Kingdom.

Lord,

Thank You for giving the perfect example of hospitality in Your Son Jesus. May we pay it forward and share the love of Christ to everyone we meet.

In Jesus' Name, Amen.

STUBBORN SPIRITUALITY

Psalm 27:14

When a little boy was younger, he wanted a mini-bike for Christmas that was a couple hundred dollars more than his parents could afford at the time. Undaunted, he spent several nights in a row in two- to three-hour intervals standing outside his bedroom door while chanting, "Mini-bike! Mini-bike! *Mini-bike!*" Eventually, his parents, wanting a peaceful rest, decided to get him the mini-bike. This was due to his persistence and not being afraid to "annoy" the person or people who could make what he wanted a reality. I'm not suggesting we act entitled to God's good grace as if we deserve all the things He generously gives us. New flash: we don't. However, while our relationship with the Father is different and deeper than an earthly relationship, like any parent-child relationship, there will be a time when the child asks something of their parents. This is not always based on selfish desire; it's an acknowledgement that we can do nothing without our parents. How much more is this true with our Heavenly Father? He wants us to come to Him with our requests in humility, but even if we don't come perfectly, He wants us to be people who desire His hand in every area of our life and be people who pray for the intangible as well as tangible. We're not often too patient when we bring a petition or request to God though. For people in our age group, maybe that's something along the lines of praying to be in a Christ-centered relationship or waiting for the right job to come along or for a classmate to come to Jesus. We can throw our hands up, feeling that a prayer not answered quickly isn't worth praying. Jesus has a different perspective though and told a parable about a persistent widow wanting justice in a manner and pleading before a callous judge.

In 1st century Israel, women held little to no power or influence in most areas of life. If you were a woman and your husband—your only source of financial stability—passed away, things would not be looking good for you. In one of Jesus' parables, a woman of that exact circumstance was seeking to settle a case before a wealthy and arrogant judge. He refused to help her, but that didn't stop her from coming to him again and again and again. Finally, the judge granted her request, not out of the goodness of his heart but just so she would quit bothering him. Waiting is easier said than done and while He doesn't grant every request right away or even every request period, the waiting period helps us rely on Him. We end up loving Him more than if we had received what we asked for, when and how we wanted it. For years, I've wanted a community that didn't just know my name but loved me and liked hanging out with me. It was difficult, and I was genuinely trying to put myself out there, but I always felt like an outsider looking in. To be honest, I felt like God was being slower than He needed to. By the grace of God, I persisted and prayed, and in that, He's provided me the privilege to be part of a community that loves Jesus and does life together. Keep being persistent in your prayers, while at the same time making sure you're actively pursuing Him in the waiting. I promise He's worth the wait, far more than any other thing you might be asking for.

God,

Grant us the grace we need to wait on whatever You are promising us individually. May we not place it on a pedestal above You, Lord.

In Jesus' Name, Amen.

DAY 5

SO MANY BROKEN PIECES, SO LITTLE GLUE

John 16:33

Among the plethora of memorable quotes from the movie *The Princess Bride*[2] is perhaps the most poignant for our Christian walk. The main protagonist of the movie, a poor farm boy, Westley, falls in love with a beautiful woman, Buttercup. Their love seems all but thwarted when he is presumably killed by the infamous criminal, the Dread Pirate Roberts. In actuality, Westley was not killed but inherited the Dread Pirate Roberts persona from the original namesake. Thinking Westley was her love's murderer, she understandably treats him with scorn. She yells to her disguised betrothed, "You mock my pain!" Without missing a beat, he replies, "Life is pain, Highness. Anyone who tells you differently is selling you something."

---

2   *The Princess Bride.* Directed by Rob Reiner, performances by Cary Elwes, Mandy Patinkin, and Wallace Shawn, 20th Century Fox, 1987.

Jesus never promises us a life of comfort and ease but the opposite. He even states in John 15 that if people hated Him, then we would naturally be hated as His followers. The exclusive claims of Christianity make Christians seem as though they are "controlling" or "bigoted." Life kind of just kicks you into a corner and makes you stay there. I mean, just turn on the news and see all the brokenness. Look around you within your life's sphere and see the brokenness. You try to do the right thing, but it just feels draining when everything around you is falling apart. You can start to wonder, "Is this God stuff even worth it?" I don't know what you're facing, but the One who knows you and the situation inside and out is bigger than any of that. Though the many little struggles we face are hard, they truly are, in the grand scheme of things, minuscule. We're not overcome because He already overcame and achieved the final victory.

God,

We praise You for the victory You graciously allow us to share. I pray You would reassure us that the troubles we face in this life are a mere blip to You and yet You see and care for us.

In Jesus' Name, Amen.

DAY 6

YOU AIN'T ALL THAT

Proverbs 16:18

No one likes a big head. If the long list of Old Testament kings getting humbled is any indication, an attitude of thinking you're the cat's pajamas doesn't work out with a holy God like ours. Nebuchadnezzar had gotten a little too big for his britches and got it twisted that he was somehow responsible for his mighty kingdom and authority. Daniel gave him a heads-up that God was having none of that and that He would make Nebuchadnezzar emulate the live-stock of the kingdom that was near and eat grass (Daniel 4:33). We have to give the Lord credit for the creative ways He acts in order to humble us. That was savage. Therein lies the problem though: we don't want to give God credit because we want to believe we carved a piece of Heaven for ourselves. We're all me-monster; otherwise, we wouldn't need to have been taught young that we're not the center of the world. If we are unwilling to work with Him to rid ourselves of the "Oh, aren't I so great?" attitude, we will never be able to truly advance His Kingdom. Remember in your highs and your lows who really deserves the glory and save yourself a trip to Old McDonald's farm.

Lord,

We confess that we're prone to diverting the glory to ourselves that rightfully belongs to You. Forgive us and transform our hearts to bow down in humility.

In Jesus' Name, Amen.

A LEAP OF FAITH INTO THE SHIRE

Isaiah 42:16

One of my good friends did a study abroad program in New Zealand. She was worried that she wasn't going to have an awesome community of believers like she did in the United States to fellowship and do life with. Nevertheless, she trusted that God would go before her and went on with it. When she arrived in Kiwi land, she and five other women in the same study abroad program were placed together. It soon became apparent to her and to the rest of the group of Christian women that they were living together seemingly by chance (*God winking*). In the coming months, deep connections were made, and my friend thrived in a community she thought she would be left without. When God calls us to do something or go somewhere, we often operate under the false assumption that things ahead are out of His control. He promises to prepare wherever He places us for whatever He has in store for us.

Emmanuel,

Thank You for going before us every step of the way. Help us trust that You don't ask us to move without first going Yourself.

In Jesus' Name, Amen.

A WORK
IN PROGRESS

1 Corinthians 6:9-11

None of us were squeaky clean when we first came to Christ. Even as we are becoming new creations who look more like Jesus, that doesn't necessarily make past and present junk in our lives any less difficult or discouraging. We think of people included in the "Bible Hero Hall of Fame" and perhaps feel inadequate because we don't have, for example, Moses' leadership, David's heart, or Paul's zeal. As inspiring as these guys are, they also had a fair amount of red in their ledger. Moses killed an Egyptian man for beating a Hebrew slave and ran away to avoid punishment. David committed adultery with a woman named Bethsheba and had her husband placed in deadly conditions in battle in order to kill him. Paul wanted to be the man known for singlehandedly crushing the early Christian movement. All of the amazing things they ended up being known for had nothing to do with their own innate abilities or skills. It had everything to do with the unexplainable, redemptive grace that God still extends today to write a different story for our lives.

Lord,

The things in our past are hard, and while we still have to face the consequences for them, we praise You for giving us a new start. May we never forget that You specialize in turning the brokenness and junk of our lives into the greatest works of art.

In Jesus' Name, Amen.

OUT-OF-WHACK HEART ALIGNMENT

Deuteronomy 5:7

Theologian John Calvin once likened the human heart to an idol factory.[3] Given how we all seem to worship something new every hour and how it's rarely the One who created us, he had a fair point. God told Moses to relay the Ten Commandments to the Israelites, and the first one was to not have any other gods before Him. He was the one who had brought them out of Egypt from Pharoah. God doesn't tolerate being "second place" to anything or anyone. That, of course, didn't stop the Israelites from creating a "god" to worship, the way many people still do today. We don't trust God will provide, and we falsely assume these things can bring us security, joy, and meaning. The thing about common idols we worship like family, money, grades, and career is that they're not bad things at all. They are good things, but as my mom likes to say, too much of any good

---

3   John Calvin, *Institutes of the Christian Religion.* Translated by Ford Lewis Battles, edited by John T. McNeill, Westminster Press, 1960.

thing is bad. Another thing is that anything other than God being the center of our lives relies on our own resources and strength to keep it there. The Israelites literally had to carry around pieces of wood and stone they falsely claimed got them out of the Red Sea. If we have to sustain the "gods" we make, they're idols and not true gods. We then need to confess and repent of the idols we have. This is often painful, but it's necessary to make God our number one. Making Jesus everything is costly, but in Him, we find our true identity and no longer look for the joy, peace, and strength that we assume these idols will bring us. Let's strive to do the hard thing of keeping these good but created things in their proper place and look to the only truly great thing: a relationship with Jesus.

Father,

Forgive us for entertaining the thought that anything other than You is worthy of being the center of our lives. Give us strength to tear down the idols in our lives even when it's painful.

In Jesus' Name, Amen.

DAY 10

AIM FOR CONSISTENCY, NOT REGULATION

Ephesians 2:8-9

Legalism says my works can obtain my salvation. Grace says Jesus' completed work on the cross was what obtained it. Legalism says I need to do all the right things to get on God's good side. Grace says He loved me undeservedly while I was still a sinner. Legalism says I need to rely on my own willpower to be holy for its own sake. Grace says I need to rely on His Spirit for the ongoing process of sanctification for love's sake. I often struggle with comparing my walk with others, spending time with Jesus out of obligation rather than love, and puffing myself up like a spiritual peacock: all symptoms of legalism, which is a sub-category of pride. Saying God's grace isn't enough for our sinfulness isn't being humble; it's just calling Him a liar. When Jesus said it was finished, He wasn't pulling your leg. He wasn't exaggerating. He meant it. Grace means getting what you don't deserve. Mercy means not getting what you deserve. If you find yourself lost, it helps to go back to the place you started and go from there. The same applies to legalism. If you start dipping your toe in it, go to the cross, where grace and justice met perfectly, and go from there.

Father,

Thank You for saving me for Your sake, not mine, and because of Your great love, not my good works. I pray that we would truly grasp how we don't deserve You in order to discover the depths of Your unending compassion.

In Jesus' Name, Amen.

LIVING WITH A LIGHTER YOKE

Matthew 11:28-30

College can be one of the most amazing experiences ever but it's also one of the busiest times in your life. Managing school, friends, family, jobs, and health is hardly a cakewalk and can easily be taxing. Additionally, trying to keep Christ as the focus while doing these things can become very exhausting very quickly and leave you burnt out. There have been moments where I've felt so over the mile-long list of things I had to do and my precious time alone with my Savior became something to check off the list. We all know life can be overwhelming, but you never truly realize how much until life seems to pummel you for ten rounds without ceasing. Jesus knows how tiring it can be just to get through the day, and He's so proud of you for continually seeking Him even though you feel depleted or drained. Exchange all your worries and anxieties for His comfort and rest. You can take any burden to Him and He'll give you His, which He promises is light.

Father,

When we have nothing in the reserves, You graciously pour Your Spirit to lift all our burdens. We praise You for that, God. We ask You to give our souls the rest they were designed for.

In Your Name, Amen.

A WORLD OF COMPROMISE

James 4:7

In the show *Spectacular Spiderman*,[4] Tombstone (a.k.a. the Big Man's criminal empire) is too massive for any normal vigilante to make a dent in it. He's far too rich and far too powerful, both in his influence and as a physical fighter. It never crosses his mind that anyone could get in the way of his "business affairs" continuing along swimmingly. That is, until Spider-Man comes along and goes beyond a mere nuisance to an actual threat to Tombstone's control over New York City. Surprisingly, Tombstone offers to pay Spider-Man for his hero work on the condition that he looks the other way on occasion: on any occasion Tombstone chooses. Peter Parker's pockets historically haven't always been the deepest, and this would help him and his Aunt May, who is struggling to provide for him. This would make his life so much easier if he looked the other way just this

---

4 *"The Invisible Hand." The Spectacular Spider-Man*, written by Matt Wayne, directed by Dave Bullock, Marvel Entertainment, 2008.

once. This is truly, unambiguously, the path of least resistance for the Wall-Crawler. He vehemently refuses, though, knowing full well the last time he looked the other way, his uncle Ben died.

When we place our faith in Jesus, we gain a target on our back for the powers of hell. Satan does everything he can to disillusion us and take us out of the battle so that his reign may continue on its borrowed time. He would love nothing more than for us to be lukewarm and compromise the responsibility given to us by our Supreme Commander of living set-apart lives for Him. He'll do or say whatever it takes for us to give up being lights for God in the darkness that's so apparent around us. With God's help, we can resist Satan's offer and strive never to look the other way when he is conquering those around us.

Gracious Protector,

Give us the eyes to notice those who desperately need to hear the Good News of Your Son. Give us the boldness and care to reach out to the hurting. May we not give in to the Enemy's pressure to look the other way.

In Jesus' Name, Amen.

"OUR" GIFTS AREN'T OURS

Psalm 18:28-36

One of the most cunning ways the Enemy tries to trip us up is by tempting us to use our God-given gifts incorrectly or for their own sake. For instance, the Lord has given me an analytical mind. The Enemy often tries to take my gift by getting me to succumb to overthinking and I end up doing nothing out of fear. Another tactic he uses is tricking us into doing what God made us for purely for its own benefit rather than for God's. For instance, Jesus and Satan both knew what Jesus was capable of and Satan challenged Him to turn stones into bread to "prove" Himself (Matthew 4:1-4). If Jesus had responded how Satan wanted Him to respond, he would have succeeded in making Him forget the purpose of every spiritual gift: to honor God. Thankfully, Jesus shows us the power of relying not only on God's strength in the battle but the invaluable resource of His Word during that encounter. With His help, we cannot only stand afterward but stand strong for the next wave of attack.

Lord,

You've gifted us with unique talents meant to draw us closer to You. We praise You for that and ask with the guiding rod of Your Word, that whatever evil plan the Enemy is forming would be thwarted.

In Jesus' Name, Amen.

DAY 14

DO SOME DIGGING

1 Samuel 16:7

After Saul dropped the ball and Israel needed a new king, Samuel was sent by God to appoint one of the sons of Jesse. He saw the stud that was Eliab and thought he was sure to be the next king. God was quick to set the prophet straight that physicality and outward appearances are minuscule factors when He decides whom He wants to use for His purposes. This verse is mostly used with the intent to encourage—and rightfully so—but it's also sobering in that our motives from within mean more to God than how we look to others. When we look at social media and see people wearing the best clothes from the best brands or having muscles that are action-figure-like, we can feel inadequate in comparison. If I'm being honest, I've valued people on the metric of how they look more times than I'm proud of. Thankfully, God's not like that and sees people how He made them. God looks inwardly at our hearts and makes them look like His Son's.

God,

Even though we can't always say the same about ourselves, it's amazing how outside appearance holds no ground about how You operate. Give us the eyes to see what You see in others and ourselves.

In Jesus' Name, Amen.

TIME PASSES LIKE THIS SENTENCE

Psalm 90:12

Time is a fleeting thing. None of us is guaranteed tomorrow or today. Jesus could come back in one century. One decade. One year. One hour. We must choose wisely how we're going to spend however much longer we have before He returns. In the story of Mary and Martha, we see two people use their time very differently. One uses it to serve others and one uses it to sit at the feet of Jesus. Both are excellent uses of time, but unless the latter takes precedence in how we spend our time, we won't be able to do the former correctly or any other important things in the timetable we're given. There are many important things for us to do before His coming, but if we let Him be the first and the last in the timetable, we'll then be able to focus on the truly important things. Not a single second will be wasted. To end with an encouragement from the band OneRepublic, "I don't know what you've been told, but time is running out, so spend it like it's gold."[5]

---

5   OneRepublic. "I Ain't Worried." *Top Gun: Maverick (Music from the Motion Picture)*, Interscope Records, 2022, https://open.spotify. com/track/4h9wh7iOZ0GGn8QVp4RAOB.

Abba,

We thank You that You help us have time for the things that are most important when we set apart time to spend with You. Help us make each moment count from the outflow of staying connected with Your Son.

In Jesus' Name, Amen.

THINK LIKE ABOVE IS DOWN HERE

Philippians 4:8

When asked by Wendy and her brothers how he's able to fly, Peter Pan is initially stumped before remembering that happy little thoughts are what power his flights through the sky. He says they, too, can fly if they think of cheerful things, and a couple of pleasant thoughts later, they're able to fly with him to Neverland.[6]

Our thoughts have a lot of power. A thought leads to an action which leads to a habit which leads to a lifestyle which leads to a character which leads to a destiny. Therefore, it's super important that our thoughts line up with God. As someone on the spectrum and with OCD, I know the futility of trying to will myself to think better thoughts. I may be able to distract myself mentally for a while, but a transformation of the mind can only come from the Spirit. When you worry about the future or think something about someone you shouldn't, ask God to renew your mind and

---

6   J. M. Barrie, *Peter and Wendy* (Hodder and Stoughton, 1911).

ask whether He wants you to think that. After that, your thoughts will be fixed on a place far better than Neverland.

Father,

There are thoughts every day that occur inside us that don't align with Your nature or Word. Help us to take each one captive and make it obedient to Christ.

In Jesus' Name, Amen.

A CRAZY CONCEPT

Zephaniah 3:17

It's possible to know intellectually of God's love but not really believe it on a heart level. Even if we do believe in our hearts that He loves us, that doesn't mean we think He likes us that much. I always thought that was the case: that He loved me dearly, but that my personality and quirks were off-putting to Him like they were to others. I assumed He *had* to love me because He was God. That could not be more wrong because the fact is He doesn't *have* to love *anyone*. He *chose* to love us and *still* chooses to love us every second. Our character and interests do change as we're conformed more and more to Jesus' image, but how God made us individually doesn't change even after being saved. I tried to act like others whom I thought God particularly enjoyed talking with and it only made me feel lonelier. Maybe you've felt the need to "impress" God and others because in the past you were the only one trying to keep the friendship afloat. Thankfully, our God is not like that. He wants nothing more than to hear from you, talk to you, and get to know you because you're His beloved child. Rejoice in the fact that God loves you and likes you.

Good Shepherd,

Thank You for genuinely enjoying whenever we spend time with each other. May we not be timid in approaching You or wonder where You stand in regard to Your love toward us.

In Jesus' Name, Amen.

EASY VS. BETTER

Matthew 7:13-14

C.S. Lewis once said, "If you want a religion that makes you feel really comfortable, I certainly don't recommend Christianity."[7] Let's be real, he's not wrong. Waking up early and prioritizing time in the Word before your screen time isn't comfortable. Speaking the truth in love at a liberal arts college isn't comfortable. Serving others while having other commitments in class and work isn't comfortable. I'm not suggesting we don't serve the One who brings ultimate comfort and peace but if our walk with Jesus costs us nothing, then chances are we're probably doing it wrong. Jesus' illustration of each road's width is very straightforward in its meaning: truly following Him is often an inconvenient and lonely privilege. Believe me, I get it. The loneliness aspect of it can make it seem like it's more trouble than it's worth, especially if you feel like you're doing it alone. The wide path truly is the path of least resistance and the ideal path if the goal is to coast through life. That path, though, only leads to mediocre spiritual growth, and I don't think

---

7   C. S. Lewis, *Mere Christianity* (Geoffrey Bles, 1952)

any of us wants that for ourselves. We want to be more like Jesus and live how He did. Rather than avoid the uncomfortable aspects of this walk, God invites us to embrace the challenges so we'll become the people we were always supposed to be. However hard the narrow path is, it's also the only one with adventure and growth, and it leads to the greatest destination we could ever hope for. What's on top of the hill of obedience is worth every hard thing so let's strap on the cleats and keep on climbing.

Lord,

Forgive us for getting caught up in the culture around us that is obsessed with maintaining personal comfort no matter the cost. Help us embrace the nitty-gritty of discipleship and exchange the comfort we try to manufacture for the comfort that makes us more like You.

In Jesus' Name, Amen.

LEAVING A LEGACY

1 Timothy 4:12

Research reveals that 70% of incoming college students who identify as Christians end up leaving their faith by the time they graduate.[8] College is basically a market of ideas, and some of them can seem a lot more appealing than Christianity. Apart from the convenience factor of other ideas compared to this narrow walk, some who choose to leave their faith have experienced genuine hurt from people who failed to model the life they have been encouraged to live. They don't know what they are missing because they've never seen it in older believers' lives. Thus, they engage in other lifestyles and worldviews. New, young believers see how easily their former fellow believers quit their former faith and then lose confidence in their own and leave, continuing the vicious cycle. First off, no one can play Christ perfectly and shouldn't be placed on a pedestal. Secondly, as preacher Adrian Rodgers pointed out, when you mistake

---

8   Zach Smith, "Family Chooses Christendom for 'Counter-Cultural Education,'" *Christendom College*, 13 Aug. 2024, https://www.christendom.edu/2024/08/13/family-chooses-christendom-for-counter-cultural-education/. Accessed 6 Apr. 2025.

a counterfeit dollar for the real deal, you don't take your life savings and burn it in fiery ashes.[9] You merely examine what is good and true, and we should, therefore, do the same in examining our faith. In this letter, Paul encourages Timothy to prove that age is irrelevant in whether someone can faithfully live for God. Our lives can show our peers who have walked away with an example they never got to witness. Earlier in the chapter, Timothy is commended to receive God-given gifts with thanks. Let's thank the people who have poured into us by taking what they've taught us and running with it. If you've never had that, find someone to mentor you and try to be that for someone else.

God,

We thank You for those whose life is a living testimony to Your power and goodness. Help us be that for those who feel hurt by those who profess Your name.

In Jesus' Name, Amen.

---

9   Adrian Rodgers, "Counterfeit Christianity," *YouTube*, uploaded by Adrian Rogers, 21 Jan. 2015, https://www.youtube.com/watch?v=makOe6OoET0. Accessed 6 Apr. 2025.

WHAT'S REALLY IMPORTANT

1 John 2:15-17

The idea of things being black and white seems to be a forgotten concept, as many would deem the things going on in the world as gray. Not to sound bleak but there is no such thing as neutrality in the spiritual realm. God is clear in His Word that there is no such thing as being on the fence about what He says is good and evil. Our commitment is either to Him or something else. Everything we do either leads us closer to God or away from Him. The Enemy knows our Creator isn't going away and that He is willing and able to sustain our heart's desires. That's why he tries to distract us with shiny objects we see all around us so we don't turn our focus to the Lord. I'm a proud nerd, but there have been a fair number of times when my focus has been more on quotes from superheroes than quotes from Scripture. The things of this world we enjoy are, in the long run, temporary, and we can't take them with us to the next realm. However exhilarating the things we're offered on earth, nothing can compare to living with God first as we were created.

Jesus,

Forgive us for turning our attention to the shiny but temporary. Help us fix our eyes on that which is unseen but eternal and give You all of our being every day.

In Jesus' Name, Amen.

COURAGE IS SCARY

Joshua 1:8-9

This is probably one of the most well-known verses in the Bible because it's very encouraging for those who struggle with fear (which is basically everyone). It's also simple for easy memorization and simple in its meaning. There really is nothing complicated about it. God commanded Joshua and the Israelites to go to the land He was about to give them based on the promise He would always be with them. That's a promise that still holds today. It cannot be stressed how straightforward and unambiguous its meaning is. That doesn't mean we aren't prone to forget that truth all the time. Human forgetfulness is one of the biggest spiritual stumbling blocks. It makes us unable to remember who God is, what He has done, and what He promises. The verse preceding this call to courage presents the solution to our innate forgetfulness: meditating, studying, and dwelling on God's Word every day. There is so much scripture in the same vein of the promise God gives to Joshua here, and we all should seek to know and memorize them when fear inevitably comes up. Scripture shouldn't just be used to comfort us but to convict us of blind spots and places where we're not stepping out in boldness. Let us hold onto His promise that He's with us always and pour ourselves into knowing the places in the Bible where He says things to that effect.

Father,

Thank You for reminding us again and again that when You ask us to go somewhere, You're right there with us holding our hand. Remind us through Your Word of Your constant Presence.

In Jesus' Name, Amen.

A FUNDAMENTAL PRINCIPLE

Colossians 1:16-17

Of the four fundamental forces that hold the universe together, gravity is the weakest. Gravity has far more significance than merely keeping us from floating into space. If the gravitational constant of the universe were altered in any way by merely one in 10^{60} parts (one followed by sixty zeroes), the universe could not function and support life. We'd be floating around aimlessly even more than we already do at times. In other words, gravity is as strong as it needs to be because it has a purpose. The purpose, as with all other aspects of nature, is to make its creative Creator known and to display a taste of His glory. Jesus is the centerpiece of creation, and everything that exists was created for His purposes, us included. We often try to make it about us and go our own way and we find out how little control we really have. Even if we include Jesus, He can be a side gig rather than our everything—as I've often treated Him and still do more than I should. When we surrender our lives to Him, the illusion of "freedom" we think we have when we go our way ends. As a result, we then experience the true freedom and joy in Him that we can't when we go our own way and try to be sovereign in our lives. Take a minute and worship the God of gravity for creating you and always being in control in a world that seems out of it every day.

Lord,

Help us realize that life is defined by You as having Jesus be front and center. Give us strength to keep the main thing the main thing.

In Jesus' Name, Amen.

DAY 23

LEADERSHIP DEFINED

1 Peter 3:8

Pete was a voice actor in the '80s and was excited to audition for the part of the main character in a cartoon. He was talking with his brother Larry about it and told him he would be a truck if he got the role. Larry laughed until Pete told him the truck was a hero. His brother, a former Marine, suddenly got serious and told him, "Peter, if you're going to be a hero, be a real hero. Don't be one of those fake Hollywood heroes who always yell and try to act tough. Be strong enough to be gentle." Those words stuck with him as he was driving to the audition and rather than proud bravado, he said these lines in a strong, yet gentle way: "My name is Optimus Prime." Since then, Peter Cullen has continued to emulate Larry's strong character while voicing the leader of the Autobots for four decades with a firm but compassionate voice.[10]

---

10   Tamera Jones, "Peter Cullen on Creating the Voice of Optimus Prime, the 'Predator,' & More in Exclusive IMAX Q&A," *Collider*, 3 Apr. 2024, https://collider.com/peter-cullen-interview-transformers-optimus-prime-predator/. Accessed 6 Apr. 2025.

Our society thinks being tough and macho means you're strong—and our God is indeed mighty—but Jesus showed that real strength means showing compassion to those who need it. Anyone who has sincerely come to Christ got there because they experienced the depth of His kindness that He gladly offers, making them want to repent and believe. God has loved us far more than we could ever imagine or deserve, and He gives us the strength to be gentle because He was and is gentle towards us.

Abba,

We praise You for dealing with us far more gently than we could ever deserve. Please help us emulate that in our relationships so You may be glorified.

In Jesus' Name, Amen.

LESSON(S) LEARNED AND APPLIED

Ecclesiastes 12:1

Chances are you're reading this having been brought up in the faith. If not, it's likely that someone older than you ministered to you and has helped you walk in your faith. College is often where you have to take everything you've learned and have been taught and decide what you are going to do with it. You can't coast off someone's faith by association anymore. We have to make a choice about how we're going to live in relation to God. A lot of incoming college students are talked out of their faith because, in the words of apologist Frank Turek, they've never been talked into it.[11] We can be overwhelmed by the newfound freedom and independence and get so caught up in the college experience that we forget the One who got us here. This isn't to say we have to get it right during this season of our lives or we're useless to the Kingdom. What I am saying

---

11 Frank Turek, *I Don't Have Enough Faith to Be an Atheist* (Crossway, 2004).

is that putting God off until after we've had our "fun" as college students wastes so much time and will negatively affect the impact we can make for the Kingdom in the long run. Please don't think I'm saying we become monks who do nothing but "spiritual" things. We should all aspire to take our faith seriously without taking ourselves seriously. God should be intertwined in all we do, whether that's having a group of people to consistently go to Bible study with, going on a road trip, or even walking to class. This is an exciting time and we should make the most of it, but let's remember to take what others have taught us to heart and start rolling with it more and more.

God,

Nothing compares to life with You at the forefront. We pray for grace and strength to keep running after You intently with all that we are.

In Jesus' Name, Amen.

IT'S DONE

Romans 8:1

Unless you're a wizard, superhero, or DeLorean-driving teen, chances are you can't go back in time and fix the mistakes of the past. It seems like no matter how well things are going now, the things of the past are just there, giving us a permanent and seemingly unfixable stain on our lives. Fortunately, the blood of Jesus wiped our past slate clean, but sometimes we wonder: did it *really*? There may be an intellectual acknowledgment of "Oh, I'm fully forgiven by God" while thinking that excludes one particular skeleton in our closet we're not proud of. There's something to be said about unconfessed sin making us feel that way. On the other hand, if it's already been confessed and repented of, why would we still feel bad about it? Partly because the Enemy tries to keep us away from the knowledge of God's magnificent grace that makes us seek Him more. By tricking us to look away from Him, he makes us get caught up in ourselves and dwell on how bad we are. We often marvel at His grace, but His holiness and hatred of sin allowed us to see His mercy on full display with Jesus voluntarily being the substitute for our punishment. He stood condemned and was declared guilty so we wouldn't. Whatever guilt the Enemy brings up from your past, tell yourself that, in the words of singer Travis Greene, "Jesus paid it all and told me I could keep the change."[12]

Jesus,

The blood washes every single stain away. Help me be bold and live in the reality that I no longer stand condemned in Your eyes.

In Jesus' Name, Amen..

---

12 Travis Greene, "Hold on Me," *Spotify*, https://open.spotify.com/ track/4PxUkKzFkpHo2mHW82jJd3. Accessed 6 Apr. 2025.

CARRYING PRECIOUS CARGO

Proverbs 18:10

When you hear the word "limousine," you probably think of spoiled executives or Hollywood celebrities who opt to be driven around by one to the grand premiere of ... *something* important. High-grade ceramic armor, bulletproof windows, and weapon-defense systems are probably not what you think comes in the typical limousine package, but such precautions are necessary when transporting the president of the United States. Nicknamed "The Beast," the custom-made Secret Service limo has been responsible for transporting our country's heads of state for decades, with each successor being updated for the best possible protection.

Saying our God is our refuge and doing something with that knowledge are very different things. The Enemy would love nothing more than to make us forget the refuge available to us in God by instilling fear of surrounding chaos. By isolating us from God, the Enemy has placed us in perfect condition to attack and severely damage our faith. When God tells us He's our fortress, He's not just saying how mighty and reliable He is. He's saying He's a fortress because that's where you put treasure. Hint, hint. He considers us treasure. God's the hip guy who brings us off the streets into His home after we put ourselves into spiritual poverty. He invites us to put up our hats and coats, take a load off, and says, "You are welcome here." But just as easily, we can seek him for protection. At the drop of a hat, God can be our warrior. How incredible is it that the God of the universe considers us so valuable that we're worth protecting?

Protector,

It's hard to grasp that despite our finiteness, You consider us precious cargo. Give us protection from the barrage of attacks we face daily from the Enemy and the world.

In Jesus' Name, Amen.

RELIABLE NAVIGATION

Psalm 119:105

So many people between the ages of 18-25 operate with no baseline of how to make decisions or go about their lives. They can kind of shoot from the hip and "guess"—a personal pet peeve of my dad. They go about their day without an objective standard, with no baseline of how to make decisions or go about their lives. This inevitably leads to them feeling drained and hopeless, thinking they have to rely on themselves without an outside source. I know there have been times I've scratched my head more than I needed to when I had God's Word available to me. As Christians, we don't have to run in circles about what we're to do when the Lord has given us the clear guidance found only in Scripture. To be clear, the Bible doesn't tell us outright, "You're meant to marry _____." or "You should be a _____." The more time we spend reading His Word and applying it, though, the more our lives will look like how God intended them to. We then have to bust the myth that we don't have time to spend with God to do that. It's not that we don't have time. It's that we're not *making* time because it's not as much of a priority as we think it is. Honestly, it hurt to write that. Please don't think this is a condemnation of what you should and shouldn't do but an invitation to what could be an essential and life-giving part of your spiritual life. Making changes in our lives in accordance with His Word is hard, but it's also the only way for freedom and direction. So, however making time for the Word looks like for you, start doing that, and you'll find the darkness fleeing really quickly

God,

Where would we be without Your truth? Help Your Word permeate our hearts and minds so that we may have a better sense of where You want us to go.

In Jesus' Name, Amen.

GOOD ACTIONS, WRONG REASONS

Isaiah 26:8

Let's be honest: following Jesus isn't what we always feel like doing. If you somehow always do, *please* feel free to tell me how you got to that point so I can be like that. There is the honeymoon stage after getting saved and then reality hits when we realize we have a Savior who's also our Lord and who calls the shots in our lives from now on. That's just plain uncomfortable at times. It's better than whatever we were doing before following Him, but it's not always easy. It's *rarely* easy. We can feel we were conned and are in a raw deal. We can try to power through the difficulty of it, and it becomes a burden or a chore rather than the joy He intended it to be. Then, what was once a genuine desire to obey and honor Him turns sour as we now do it with gritted teeth or annoyed reluctance rather than out of a deep love for God. Jesus pointed to the Pharisees in fulfillment of the prophecy from Isaiah—You hypocrites! Isaiah was right when he prophesied about you:"'These people honor me with their lips, but their hearts are far from me. They worship me in vain; their teachings are merely human rules.'" (Matthew 15:7-9). It's not just about what we are doing for God but *why* we are doing it. Before we do anything for Him with our hands, He first and foremost wants our hearts. He wants our singular desire to glorify Him in all we do, not willfully out of pride but willingly out of love. He wants us to trust that His way is better and more satisfying and that by obeying Him, we will never be in lack. Having the right motivations doesn't happen overnight; it happens through the day-to-day process of wanting Him over anything for His sake rather than our own. It won't get any easier, and there are days I wonder why I keep at it. Thankfully, He promises that when we carry His yoke, that it is easy and His burden is light.

Lord,

Forgive us for wanting to settle for something numbing and comfortable as opposed to the growth we can only experience through the pain that comes with discipleship. Remind us that life is only worth living when it's lived for You.

In Jesus' Name, Amen.

REJOICING AND WEEPING

John 11:35

While we now have a life of exuberant joy in Jesus, that doesn't mean there won't be times when we'll just feel downright distraught or *"done"* with everything. Sadness is not something we get a free pass from once we're saved. In fact, the knowledge we gain of the place where He will wipe away every tear can make us more depressed that the tears we cry here keep going and going and going. We feel like the promise of hope and peace and joy even in the hard things was just a sales pitch into the Kingdom. If we allow it, our minds can soon become consumed with thoughts that God doesn't see us when we're down and that if He does, He doesn't care. Jesus was and still is one-hundred-percent God, but He was also a human who faced human troubles. In this short verse, we see Jesus working through the death of his dear friend Lazarus by accepting the sadness of the event and allowing Himself to cry. He knew what He was going to do, but our Lord still recognized that this

THE RIGHT ROCK: 100 DAY DEVOTIONAL

was a heavy moment. We shouldn't stay stuck in despair indefinitely, but we need to allow ourselves to feel sad; otherwise, any future joy will be cheap. Take comfort in your sorrow that Jesus loved you enough to bear your pains, big and small. Life will still be painful, but His light will reign in the end. In the words of Ellie Holcomb and Bear Rinehart, "Got a lot of bad days still coming our way but a sweet ever-after."[13]

Father,

Thank You for being our eternal shoulder to cry on. Remind us to bring all our sorrow, hurt, and shame to you knowing you experienced it already through Your Son.

In Jesus' Name, Amen.

---

13 Ellie Holcomb and Bear Rinehart, "Sweet Ever After," *Spotify*, https://open.spotify.com/track/0zdLZywwUVyg8xnzzxgDBP. Accessed 6 Apr. 2025.

THE RIGHT INQUIRIES

Job 19:25-27

"Is this *really* true? Or am I just wasting my time?" I've often asked that in regard to my beliefs. Doubts about God's existence have definitely crept in from time to time on whether the end of my life is when eternity in glory begins or just the end of a good run before sleeping in the dirt forever. As someone on the spectrum, "just have faith" doesn't always work for me. I have more difficulty than most turning off my inner investigator. That's not necessarily a bad thing, but it can certainly lead to a lot of overthinking rather than participating in what God wants me to do at the moment. So many people in their late teens or early 20s leave the faith because they have questions and are discouraged from asking them. Well-meaning Christians can be more focused on trying to prove wrong the people who question or put them in their place at the cost of making them feel seen and heard and that truth-seeking questions are welcome. Most people would think their doubting problems would end if they heard a literal voice from Heaven. Those people seem to forget that John the Baptist, the person who literally *heard* a voice from Heaven and whom Jesus declared as the greatest in the Kingdom of Heaven, had his doubts, too. When John sent his disciples to ask Jesus if He was the person He said He was, Jesus responded with patience and understanding and told them to tell John of the tangible evidence. He's not intimidated by our doubts but invites us to press into Him in our questioning. I certainly encourage you to do your own research to better explain to others why you believe what you believe. Often, though, what we're doubting is not always intellectual but emotional. "Does God really love me?" "Why would he let this horrible thing happen?" We can question His goodness and faithfulness because our emotions are just so heavy. Feelings, as powerful as they may seem, aren't facts. They're subjective and always changing, but the facts of who Jesus is and what His character is like is certain. You might not always feel confident, but know your hope of meeting your Savior face-to-face is certain.

God,

Thank You for not being intimidated by our doubts and wanting to be near us even when we doubt Your goodness. Help us ask these questions while still keeping in mind that the answer is always more of You in our lives.

In Jesus' Name, Amen.

GROWING UP, GROWING WIDE, AND GROWING DEEP

2 Peter 3:17-18

In *Rocky III*,[14] after beating Apollo Creed in an intense re-match, Rocky Balboa goes from being the "People's Champion" to being the actual world heavyweight boxing champion. Balboa goes from rags to riches and gets pretty used to it, much to his trainer Mickey's chagrin. He soon, though, grows complacent in his life of luxury, and a few years of not being challenged by elites like Apollo Creed influence his edge for the worst. As a result, when the "wrecking machine" known as Clubber Lang comes on the scene, he is beaten quite convincingly because he got "civilized," the worst thing that can happen to a fighter. Surprisingly, Apollo offers to train the Philadelphian boxer for a rematch

---

14 *Rocky III*. Directed by Sylvester Stallone, performances by Sylvester Stallone, Carl Weathers, Mr. T, and Talia Shire, MGM, 1982.

against Lang after Mickey passes. He has to learn an entirely different style of fighting to regain the killer instinct he once had fighting Creed. The training is hard, but it pays off as he is able to knock down Clubber Lang in their second bout and regain the championship.

As believers, we need to make sure we're never too comfortable with where we are in our relationship with Christ. Celebrating where God has grown us is awesome, but He's not done yet, and we shouldn't be done either. I know I'm guilty of taking a victory lap longer than I should as opposed to continuing to run, sharper and more focused. It's so easy to just settle and hover at our current spiritual level. God never forcibly twists our arm to do something but patiently invites us to take it a step deeper. Complacency is so easy to partake in but it prevents the ongoing adventure of doing life with Jesus from being as impactful or transforming as it could be. There's always more to learn and always more to accomplish for His glory. With His Spirit's help, we can maintain the "eye of the tiger" in this ongoing daily battle against Satan.

Lord,

Your invitation to a deeper everything really is going to shape us in ways that make us squirm at times. We still want it, though, and desire to be more effective in whatever it is You're asking us to do.

In Jesus' Name, Amen.

PARASITES

2 Corinthians 11:14

It's been long thought that the tiny oxpecker helped out large African grass-grazing mammals by cleaning off the animal's ticks while getting a meal, a type of mutualistic relationship commonly seen in nature. However, some recent research shows that these interactions may not be as "buddy-buddy" as they seem on the surface. While the oxpecker removes ticks, it continues to peck long after the ticks have been removed and causes new bleeding wounds in the animal they're on. Many animals have caught on to this rather intrusive pecking and trying to shake them off, recognizing no tick removal is worth being intruded upon while eating breakfast.

In this letter, Paul describes to the church false teachers whose ill effects are not merely bad in the long run (although they are). They're being used knowingly or not by the Enemy to make something somewhat resembling the gospel to keep people happy, comfortable, and, as the Enemy really desires, lukewarm. It's hard to let go if something makes your life more convenient and satisfying, but it amounts to junk food and can't truly sustain your spiritual growth. Furthermore, it would be intellectually dishonest and hard-hearted for us to be willing to go along with a teaching we know is not in line with God's Word. The Enemy can't make his junk not junk, but he can certainly trick us into thinking when we go along with him that we're getting a Ferrari. All we're getting is a lemon. When a teaching or idea doesn't seem to align with God's Word, don't ignore that feeling. Press into the Holy Spirit and do your own research. Ask trusted, seasoned believers who have experience checking themselves to see what's true and what isn't. Through Scripture and prayer, you can shake off any false idea meant to lead you away from God's loving arms.

Holy Spirit,

Convict us of the ideas we assume are from Your Word that are really not. Help us discern what's true so that we may know that where the Spirit of the Lord is, there is freedom.

In Jesus' Name, Amen.

DAY 33

A HEAVENLY HOPE

Romans 15:13

In the critically acclaimed film *Shawshank Redemption*,[15] bank manager Andry Dufresne is found guilty of murdering his cheating wife and her lover by way of ammunition. The only problem is, he didn't do it, and when he did have thoughts of ending both of their lives, he backed out and threw his gun into the lake, which was a different gun than the one that shot his wife. He's sent to Shawshank State Prison, which is ruled with an iron fist by the hypocritical religious warden whose number two is the scourge of all prisoners there. In a deep pit such as this, it would have made sense for Dufresne to give up hope entirely. He doesn't give in to despair, though, and the actions he takes based on his hope spread to the other prisoners, including old con Ellis "Red" Redding, whose sentiment was once, "Hope is a dangerous thing; hope can drive a man insane." Our hope is not in the circumstances: it's in the hope that because Jesus rose, we can rise from any disappointment

---

15   *The Shawshank Redemption.* Directed by Frank Darabont.
Performances by Tim Robbins, Morgan Freeman, Bob Gunton, and
Clancy Brown, Columbia Pictures, 1994.

or crushed dream. This hope isn't a passive belief of something that'll happen but something on which to base our actions going forward. Dufresne gives two options about how to live life: "Get busy living or get busy dying." In light of this great hope, let's choose the former.

God,

You know life can beat us down to our knees. Help us realize that often, it's only from that place that we realize our need for You to give us eternal hope. Fill us with hope in every situation, whether on the mountain or in the valley.

In Jesus' Name, Amen.

FEELING [BLANK]? PRAY.

Psalm 27:8

The excuse of having too much to do to be able to pray doesn't really work if you take a moment to consider that Jesus was the busiest man alive and yet still made time to pray. He wouldn't have been as attentive to the voice of His Father and the proper steps to take in His ministry if He didn't take time for the mystery of prayer. Another reason He prayed was that, as a rabbi, He expected his students to model His way of life, which was really one long conversation with God. My mind's gears tend to spin a thousand miles per second, but even if you're not on the spectrum, focusing during prayer can be really difficult. It must also be considered that we're worried we won't sound right. One other anxious thought that keeps us from praying is that we're not praying to anyone but instead talking to the sky. We can get discouraged until we remember the fact that Jesus loves to talk to us. He loves hearing our requests to Him, wants us to know true joy through gratitude, and for us to take every hurt and give it to Him in prayer. Instead of seeing prayer as something we have to do or a good thing we should do, let's reframe it as something we get to do. May we always remember what a privilege it is to commune with Jesus every day.

Father,

Forgive us for living hurried lives and believing the lie that we don't have time to talk to You and be in Your Presence. Help us realign our lives to seek You and be more aware of the moments where we're invited to talk to You.

In Jesus' Name, Amen.

YOU DON'T PICK YOUR FAMILY

2 Timothy 2:22

I think most of us would say we like our alone time but don't like being lonely. That's by design (His design) for humanity. Simply put, we weren't meant to do life alone. We were created primarily to be in a relationship with God, but we're also created to have community with others. When we are not involved in friendships with fellow believers, we're missing out on what God created. I can personally attest that being in isolation, voluntarily or involuntarily, will negatively affect your health physically, mentally, and spiritually. Another kicker is that if we are desperate for fellowship, we'll unwittingly lower our God-given standards with whom we surround ourselves. It's not rocket science that we become like someone else the more we hang out with them. I'm not suggesting we cut off all contact with non-Christians, as we cannot be salt and light to others if we don't engage with them. I've met some very kind non-Christians who know how to love well. The difference, though, between them and my Christian friends is noticeable. Your friends who are your brothers and sisters in Christ can and will help you in your walk more than you can imagine. Therefore, be intentional to surround yourself with people who will do life with you and remind you of the reason you do life in the first place.

Abba,

You place the lonely in families because You knew we needed each other. Help us be mindful of the company we choose to surround ourselves with and seek deeper friendship with those who love You and want to know You more.

In Jesus' Name, Amen.

DAY 36

FIRST MATE
WISDOM

Proverbs 2:6

In the '60s sitcom *Gilligan's Island*,[16] the captain and his first mate, along with their passengers, are trapped as castaways on an uninhabited tropical island with no access to the mainland. The series follows the group's hijinks and attempts to escape from the island. One castaway is a professor who is so brilliant he once made a lie-detecting device out of coconuts. For some reason, though, it's incredibly vexing for him to fix a two-foot hole in a boat.

Jesus' interactions with the smart-aleck Pharisees show that you can be intelligent and still not be that bright. There is a lot to be gained by studying a lot of facts and knowing a thing or two about important topics. However, unless we act on what we have learned or rely on God to help us apply the knowledge, it won't really matter if we have a master's degree in Intellectual Jargon. We'll still be full of hot air and

---

16 Sherwood Schwartz, creator, *Gilligan's Island*, CBS Productions, 1964–1967.

be totally void of any meaningful substance, much like a majority of the religious teachers of Jesus' day. When we go to God to help us practically put into practice the knowledge He's given us, we can avoid acting like wise guys and just be wise.

Lord,

Thank You for wanting us to reach out for wisdom in the confusing world we live in. Grant us wisdom that's applicable, true, and points back to You in whatever situation we are in.

In Jesus' Name, Amen.

BOAST WELL

Jeremiah 9:23-24

I think we've all boasted about ourselves at least once in the past. I know I have and still have a bad habit of doing it sometimes. I can do all the right things for all the wrong reasons. I can see how far I've come and indulge in patting myself on the back, saying, "Yeah, I'm the bees' knees." What makes this boasting about ourselves unwarranted is that we can't live up to our own hype. We're not as smart, capable, or noble as we think we are, as much as we want to present ourselves better than we probably are. I'm not trying to undermine the natural gifts and talents God has given us. I'm simply pointing out that when we see the toolset He's equipped us with as anything more important than tools for His glory, it becomes a problem. Furthermore, unless any statement we say about ourselves or our abilities is filtered through God's unmerited grace and truth, it'll end up on either extreme on the spectrum of big ego or lack of ego, which are both states of mind that will lead to pride. We're not more or less important, and that's a hard thing to grasp and understand. The only thing about ourselves we're told to boast about is our weaknesses, as Paul says in the twelfth chapter of 2 Corinthians. This is rather countercultural when we are accustomed to boasting about how we aced the job interview, how fruitful a ministry is, and just how many people like us. The apostle Paul states that it is in our weakness that He is strong, and what an amazing thing it is that our God has it all together when we feel pressured by the culture around us to keep all our ducks in order. There is ironically more joy and confidence in boasting of how kind, just, and mighty our God is than we could ever experience when we indulge in self-promoting.

God,

Your love and power prove You alone are worthy of worship. May we boast in nothing else other than what You did for us on the cross.

In Jesus' Name, Amen.

HOW TO BE CONTENT

Nehemiah 8:10

The pressures athletes deal with are very reminiscent of the pressure in our lives as Christians; this is probably one reason our walk is compared to that of an athlete competing. Softball is no exception, as the Oklahoma Sooners womens softball team has certainly broken a sweat at maintaining their record-breaking streak. After winning the NCAA Division 1 championship, an ESPN reporter asked how they could be so joyful despite the high demands of the game. Grace Turk (then Lyons), the captain of the team, answered, "The only way you can have a joy that doesn't fade away is from the Lord. And any other type of joy is actually happiness that comes from circumstances." Another player concurred and stated while pointing up, "Eyes up. We're really fixing our eyes on Christ."[17] That's what separates the joy of the Lord from anything else: it's available even when the test grade isn't what we hoped. It's available

---

17   Grace Turk, personal interview, 6 June 2023.

when we don't get the class we wanted. It's available when a friendship doesn't work out. That isn't to say that those things are *bad*, per se. I once heard it said that we all have a God-shaped hole in our heart, and I'll give you three guesses what can fill it. If our happiness is dependent on things going all sunshine and rainbows, it's a good indicator *we've* grown shallow as believers and people. As difficult as hard times can be, they're an opportunity to see how the Spirit is working in us, as we can have joy and peace irrespective of whether things go our way. It also really grinds the Enemy's gears when we rejoice in the Lord even in our troubles and get others' attention on how we don't let stuff get to us knowing the ultimate victory has already been won by Jesus. You can access this unchanging joy daily and shine a light on those living without it.

Jesus,

You offer joy that's possible on the good days, bad days, and everything in between. Fill us completely with this joy and may we be bold in telling others where we derive it from.

In Jesus' Name, Amen.

UNO REVERSE CARD

Romans 8:28

We take comfort that God can turn any hardship or difficulty around until we actually have to deal with them and the consequences that come with them. I'll be real: I'd much rather praise God when things are going dandy than when it's just one hard thing after another. Most of us would. However, if we only experienced one pleasant thing after another and that was the only time we praised God, we would turn into rather shallow people, and our commitment to Him would be fair-weather at best. I don't pretend to know why God allows every bad thing to happen but if we don't know suffering, then we probably would think we didn't need Him. Oftentimes, it's when people are at their lowest that they call out to God, not when they're on cloud nine. His deep love redeeming any hard thing makes us deeper people with deeper longing for more of Him. We also need to remember that even if what we endure isn't good, He never ceases to be good and is literally incapable of doing anything that is bad for us in the long run. Our God is a strategic genius and is always thinking five steps ahead of the Enemy's plan for harm. Rest in the fact that the hard thing you're dealing with is not irredeemable from God turning it around for your good and His glory.

Father,

Some things in our life just suck and still suck even though You never stop being good. Give us patience to see it's not the end and You're not done with us yet.

In Jesus' Name, Amen.

HE KEEPS HIS PROMISES, NOT OURS

Numbers 23:19

There are few things in the world more binding than a pinky promise. Peter says in his first letter that God can afford to make such great promises because of His divine nature. Whatever He promises us doesn't always happen at the pace we would like, though. If we've had our trust violated enough, it can make us question whether or not He's really trustworthy. I always figured He promised me a friend or two to connect with, but for years, it was really hard. After sharing my struggles with an autism support group, we talked about how those on the spectrum can have difficulty making meaningful connections with others. Feeling a little discouraged, I prayed on my knees that God would provide me with a good roommate and give me the grace I needed to be a good friend and roommate in return. I trusted that He would do whatever was in His will even if it wasn't on my timing. The *very next day* during school, I got a text from a guy I had a 96% match with on the housing app. I talked with the guy and found he had just responded to a response I did last month. When he saw I responded to his late response immediately, he told me it felt ordained by God. To say we hit it off well is a tremendous understatement. I just asked God for a roommate who was cordial and had a reasonable sleep schedule. I didn't know this guy would be the best roommate I could ever hope for, much less my best friend and amazing brother in Christ. If God promises something and you don't have it, it just means He's growing you as He's getting it ready for you. If He didn't promise it, it just means He has something better for you. Either way, keep holding Him to His pinky swear.

Lord,

You never promise us every single thing our hearts desire: just what we really need because You love us and know what's best. Remind us that it's ok to keep asking for Your promises to come to fruition and to hold You to them because You never ever break them.

In Jesus' Name, Amen.

FREEDOM IN FAILURE

Luke 18:14

No one likes to confess when they've fallen short or messed up. It's just human nature, going back to where Adam and Eve tried to point the finger elsewhere to avoid taking responsibility for their sin. Chances are the highlight reel of someone else's Instagram isn't the complete picture, as much as you think and as much they want you to think it is. What's also in human nature is for others to be authentic. We can look at someone else's seemingly "pitch-perfect" life waiting for them to fail, which is hardly Christ-like, so we don't feel as bad about our mess-ups. This is still a prideful state of mind and severely missing the point of how we all fall short against a holy and awesome God like ours. I'm often guilty of trying to make myself seem super spiritual and make it appear I have it all together compared to my peers. I got put in my place when someone I deeply admire, yet compared myself to, shared his struggles and how he relied on God's grace when he fell. His mess-up didn't make me think less of him but rather more, because he could admit it and keep pressing in on God's grace. Oftentimes, people turned off by Christianity get to that point when the "Christians" in their life don't own their mistakes. Let's start getting real about our trip-ups to God and see how our vulnerability honors Him and gives others space to be honest about their stumbling.

God,

Search our hearts and expose the areas that don't line up with Your character or Word. Forgive us for being spiritual peacocks and help us humble ourselves so that You get the glory.

In Jesus' Name, Amen.

COMMUNITY ACCORDING TO CHILD PLAYTHINGS

1 Thessalonians 5:11

When Buzz Lightyear arrives in Andy's room, every toy is amazed by his features as a space toy, much to Sheriff Woody's chagrin and jealousy. He's frustrated because Buzz has seemingly taken his spot as Andy's favorite toy and because Buzz is genuinely convinced he is a Space Ranger. They're at odds until they're taken by Andy's neighbor Sid, who is every toy's worst nightmare. Buzz faces immense shock when he discovers through a commercial his origin is not found in the stars but in Taiwan. He falls into deep despair when faced with the truth. He might have stayed in that sadness indefinitely had Woody not risen above himself and encouraged Buzz on what an awesome responsibility they as toys have. From this experience, Woody and Buzz become the best of friends and their friendship throughout the *Toy Story*[18] franchise is one of building each other up.

As believers, we need to sit with each other in our grief and help one another process the pain. We must do this by not letting the other person stay there too long without reminding them of God's faithfulness. It's an amazing thing to encourage others because while we're encouraging them, we're being encouraged by our encouragement in an encouraging cycle. So, the next time you see someone working on something but don't know how it will turn out or being down on themselves, say to them, "You've got a friend in me."

Holy Spirit,

You welcome us with open arms and call us Your friends when we've been anything but that to You. Please grant us wisdom on how to better reflect You in our relationships.

In Jesus' Name, Amen.

---

18 *Toy Story*. Directed by John Lasseter, performances by Tom Hanks, Tim Allen, and Wallace Shawn, Pixar Animation Studios, 1995.

ASSEMBLED,
WE ARE STRONG

Romans 12:4-8

I've always been partial to the Avengers[19] over the Justice League,[20] partly because the roster of the former is not as overpowered as the latter, which gets boring for meaningful storytelling. Marvel's Earth's mightiest heroes each provide a unique set of abilities and skills that make them able to take on a variety of missions. Hawkeye is not destroying armies with one blow but a mighty warrior like Thor can. Iron Man's one-man party attitude would make him ineffective in calling the shots so that's why you need a leader in Captain America. Hulk's about as subtle as a gamma bomb, making an elite spy and assassin in the Black Widow necessary in missions that require stealth. Each does

---

19 *The Avengers*. Directed by Joss Whedon, performances by Robert Downey Jr., Tom Hiddleston, Chris Evans, and Mark Ruffalo, Walt Disney Studios Motion Pictures, 2012.

20 *Justice League*. Directed by Zack Snyder, performances by Ben Affleck, Gal Gadot, Jason Momoa, and Ezra Miller, Warner Bros., 2017.

something the other can't and covers their weak points in order to better fulfill the team's purpose.

If we're being honest, we compare our God-given talents with those of others because we don't like what He made us good at. Even if we appreciate what He blessed us with, we can throw a pity party as it's not as good as when "so-and-so" does the same thing. There's immense freedom in knowing that it's not about us: it's about Him. He didn't give us these talents to do whatever we want and for our own benefit. He gave them trusting that we would use them to build His Kingdom and work alongside other believers with their talents. If you think you don't have a talent, remember that God has uniquely blessed you in a way that no one else can do what you do. The blessings others have received don't lessen yours but complement one another's for His glory.

Lord,

We thank You for making each of us gifted and equipping us for the task You give each one of us. We pray for You to give us a vision of how You're inviting us to partner with one another and further Your Kingdom.

In Jesus' Name, Amen.

EVERYTHING PLUS ONE IS STILL EVERYTHING

Psalm 23:1

In terms of Marvin Gaye and Tammi Terrell duets, it doesn't get much better than "Ain't No Mountain High Enough."[21] However, "You're All I Need to Get By"[22] isn't too bad, either, with each singer reflecting the other is all they need to depend on. A lot of trouble could be avoided if we just trusted that God alone can provide whatever it is we're looking for instead of going to other places for it. Sin is a picture of what not depending on or trusting in God looks like. Our desires always reflect a deeper longing for something, and it doesn't matter what that something is: God is able and willing to satisfy it in Him. If we desire to date someone, what we really want is intimacy with another person, which is perfectly found in a relationship with Christ. If we want a certain job, what we really want is fulfillment and security,

---

21 Marvin Gaye and Tammi Terrell, "Ain't No Mountain High Enough," *United*, Tamla Records, 1967.

22 Marvin Gaye and Tammi Terrell, "You're All I Need to Get By," *You're All I Need*, Tamla Records, 1968.

which is perfectly found in walking in step with God's will for your life. It's totally acceptable to ask things like these from God but we need to ask with the mindset of knowing He'll fulfill every desire in Himself. David was a shepherd before he became king of Israel so his connection to how a shepherd protects and provides for his flock isn't a coincidence. It was him drawing from his life experience to show us with God's help, He's all that he needed to get by.

Lord,

With You, there is never a lack but it often doesn't feel that way. Help us see how You aren't just fulfilling all our needs but surpassing them.

In Jesus' Name, Amen.

STOP DRINKING THE POISON

Colossians 3:13

C.S. Lewis quite accurately pointed out that "everyone thinks forgiveness is a lovely idea until they have something to forgive."[23] I'm not trying to come down with judgment at all. Believe me, I've been there. Being hurt by someone else's action sucks, and it's accurate to say thinking about forgiving is way easier than the actual practice of forgiving someone for hurting you. Holding a grudge gets in the way of our spiritual growth and often in small ways we probably wouldn't otherwise notice. Unforgiveness makes us bitter and defensive at not just the person who wronged us but to everyone in general. Unforgiveness puts us in a state of self-centeredness where all our mind dwells on is how we've been wronged. Unforgiveness even severs the connection we have with God in prayer, as Jesus even said He won't forgive those who won't forgive. The simple fact is we're called to forgive because we've been forgiven.

---

23 C. S. Lewis, *Mere Christianity* (Geoffrey Bles, 1952), p. 104.

91

That doesn't mean the relationship has to be restored if the person is continually unrepentant. Forgiveness is a gift we're supposed to give but trust is something that has to be earned by the offending party. It was once said that holding onto a grudge was like drinking poison and expecting the other person to die. Forgiving others is hard, but unless we realize the boundless grace we've been given undeservedly, we'll never freely or gladly give that same grace to others.

Jesus,

It's insane to withhold forgiveness from someone when we've literally been showered by grace from You. Help us realize that Your forgiveness doesn't stop with us but it spreads as we forgive like You do.

In Jesus' Name, Amen.

DAY 46

LISTEN

Ecclesiastes 5:2

Two ears. One mouth. That's what my mom always says in regard to the proportion people should listen to compared to how much they speak. I know for a fact I don't live by that recommended ratio, but it's still a good principle to remember when we're trying to put the words in our mouths at the same rate we heard them in our head. We're often in such a rush to pray in our busy schedules because "it's the Christian thing to do" that we don't let God get a single word in. I'm not suggesting we shouldn't bring our petitions to God, but prayer isn't a list of things we'd like God to fix in our life. It's a life-long conversation with Jesus and as is the case in any meaningful conversation, prayer involves taking turns: listening and speaking. Silence can be quite terrifying, if I'm being totally honest. The worry of whether something I hear is not from God but just a random thought in my head has come up before. The danger of trying to come up with things to say is that the large surplus of things we say is just fluff and not honoring the King of Glory. Jesus spent his life listening to God, and while we may not hear an audible voice, letting God get the first and last word will do wonders in our prayer life.

Abba,

We so often tell You to keep up when we should be slowing down so we can hear what You're saying. Give us ears to hear You and abide more deeply.

In Jesus' Name, Amen.

WHATEVER YOU DO, SHARE THIS LIFE AND TREASURE

Isaiah 52:7

Right before His ascension to Heaven, Jesus' disciples were instructed by their Master to go and make more followers of Him. That wasn't something He commanded only to His apostles: Jesus expects us to do it today. Sharing our faith can be nerve-wracking, to say the least. I know the idea of telling others about Jesus can make me anxious more than it should. We can get nervous about sharing our faith because we're afraid people will think we're "weird." For me, truth is super important, and telling others the truth is also important to me, so I want to make sure when I tell them about Jesus, it's because He's nothing less than the real deal. If we're truly serious about our faith, we should want to tell others the reason for the hope we have. It's truly the best news ever that we can be forgiven for our sins no matter what we've done and that if we accept Him, we'll be in glory with Him forever. Plus, if we love others, we'll tell them about the condition of sin we're all diagnosed with at birth and who the Doctor is. Paul reminds us in Philippians 2 that everyone is going to acknowledge who Jesus is in the end, and unfortunately, a lot of people will be standing on the opposite side of Him doing that. We don't need to be intimidated by ministering to our peers because Jesus promises to be with us every step of the way. It's a relief to know it's not on me to save people and He made us all to be intentional in our own specific ways. It's encouraging to know we don't need to be masters of rhetoric to put in a good word about Jesus. It's as easy as willingly opening our mouths and letting Him speak through us.

Emmanuel,

It's hard to be bold for You, but it's worth it. It's so worth it. Help us not treat people like projects but love them in a way that points them to You simply because that's the outflow of our lives.

In Jesus' Name, Amen.

IT WILL SET YOU FREE AND TICK YOU OFF

Proverbs 12:17

The truth often hurts. The truth of how we're really feeling when we tell everyone we're fine can hurt. The truth of the state of a relationship you poured so much of yourself into can hurt. The truth of the difficult struggles you're facing academically, mentally, and spiritually can hurt. When the truth seems to bring nothing but pain, little white lies that appear to be effective and harmless can seem very appealing. Minor exaggerations or half-truths initially bode well, but the more our lips speak contrary to the Spirit of truth inside of us, it gives a lot of room for the Enemy to do his dirty work. Lies also limit the intimacy we get to experience with God and others. Between an inconvenient truth and a convenient lie, the latter's always going to be easier to swallow than the former. The most unnerving truth of all is that none of us deserve His love. We didn't somehow get our act together and He decided we were worth keeping around because of our own merit. He stepped down to our level and lived the perfect life we never could and made us right with Himself because that's just the kind of God He is. The amount of freedom we experience in our lives is directly proportional to how honest we are with ourselves, others, and God. Let's strive to know the truth of God's Word that Jesus promised will set us free.

Lord,

Lies can't exist in Your Presence. They just can't. Help us be truth tellers about who You are and what You have to say about the world and all that lies in it.

In Jesus' Name, Amen.

DEAD WEIGHT

Hebrews 12:1-2

In *Finding Nemo*,[24] Marlin is a resident clownfish from the Great Barrier Reef who is immensely overprotective of his son Nemo. He has good reason to be, as a barracuda devoured his wife Coral and the rest of his unborn offspring, leaving only Nemo who has a shriveled fin because of the attack. This hinders Marlin's belief that Nemo is capable of great things, and their relationship is strained as a result. Things take a turn for the worse when Nemo is taken by scuba divers after arguing with his father. A forgetful blue tang called Dory crosses paths with Marlin and enlists herself in the journey to find Nemo. She encourages the pessimistic clownfish to "just keep swimming" when life gets you down. He soon takes this to heart about himself and his son's capability. Eventually, he pays it forward by instructing the fish trapped in a net with Dory to "just keep swimming" to save her. We all have things slowing us down from running this race. It could be guilt from a past

---

24 *Finding Nemo*. Directed by Andrew Stanton, performances by Albert Brooks, Ellen DeGeneres, Willem Dafoe, and Geoffrey Rush, Pixar Animation Studios, 2003.

sin that's been forgiven. It could be guilt from the sin currently in your life. It could be the pain of a past hurt that remains hurting. Whatever it may be, know that God has enabled us through His Son to be able to get rid of the dead weight in our lives and run boldly to His care. He's calling us to run the way He's already marked out for us so we're not guessing where or how to run. With His help, we can overcome any stumbling block, past or present, and keep moving forward to a place like P. Sherman 42 Wallaby Way Sydney from the movie and beyond.

God,

The past always seems to cast a deep shadow, but the deepness You offer in Your comforting shade is more so. May the things holding us back from You be cast out so we can move forward more freely as we run with purpose.

In Jesus' Name, Amen.

REPTILE-HUNTING WISDOM

James 1:5-8

My German Shorthaired Pointer, Max, is everyone's friend. He's been my Bible study partner for years, often sitting next to me on the couch. He has to know where I am at all times or he gets nervous. He's my best buddy, but he's also the biggest goober I know. Max has a bad habit of trying to fit shelled reptiles far too wide to even fit in his mouth into his tummy. Usually, the process of getting a turtle out of his mouth lasts a few minutes, but I recall one instance where it was stuck for over half an hour. Master Splinter's pupil was lodged in there so Max couldn't have let him go even if he wanted to. Eventually, we got it loose but he still held the turtle in his mouth, and if he continued to have it in his mouth, Max would've gotten seriously hurt or worse. I prayed to God for wisdom in what to do and I suddenly got the idea to grab pieces of cheese from the refrigerator. I made a trail that distracted Max long enough for him to drop the turtle, and Dad was able to get it away as I held

Max. Making wise choices is always important and this time in our lives is no exception. How amazing that through His Word and His Spirit, God gives us wisdom for all situations, not excluding dislodging a turtle from a goofball's mouth.

Holy Spirit,

We know You don't just want to communicate when we need something. That being said, You want to hear every request, big or small. Give us the confidence to approach you for whatever petition we have.

In Jesus' Name, Amen.

KEEP A RECORD

Psalm 111:2-4

If we took time to remember all we've been through, we would realize how often God has been throughout all of it. It's rare in our busy and rushing culture that we remember who He is and who we are in Him. Our circumstances can affect our perception of God and make us amnesiac to what's grounded in reality. If we're facing a hardship that is seemingly too much to bear, we'll forget the faithfulness He showed when we were facing a previous hardship. If things are going peachy keen, we can get it twisted that it's like that because we, by our own merits, have the skills that pay the bills. Either extreme is not helpful in our relationship with Him and keeps us from the obedience He desires. Moses exhorted the Israelites to remember God and who He was and still is. They needed to remember He was the one who brought them out of Egypt. They needed to remember He parted the Red Sea. They needed to remember that He watched over and sustained them for forty years in the wilderness. There were painful things they were called to remember, such as their disobedience, but unless they recalled where they went wrong, they wouldn't learn. When you see God clearly working in your life, don't just thank Him for it but make every effort to respond to His promises as Peter said in his second book. We shouldn't live in the past but having memories of Him showing up helps inspire us to obey now and in the future. Keep His good acts in your memory base—remember He's still faithful and let that inspire your faithfulness going forward.

God,

Life's ups and downs have a way of making us forget who You are in our lives. Remind us of Your past faithfulness and remember that who You were then is who You are now and who You'll always be.

In Jesus' Name, Amen.

YOU FELL HARD. WHAT NOW?

Proverbs 24:16

Paul Hewson a.k.a. "Bono," the lead singer of the Irish rock band U2, once said that his "heroes are the ones who survived doing it wrong, who made mistakes, but recovered from them."[25] The fact is, everyone makes mistakes. *Everyone.* We know this because Paul says in Romans 3:23 (NIV), "For all have sinned and fall short of the glory of God." Even if you've never heard of that verse, you would agree with this simply because in the past, that's been your lived experience. Our failures can bring us down to dangerous levels to the point where we start asking, "What's the point of trying to do better?" There is a time and place for godly sorrow that leads to repentance, but throwing a pity party for ourselves doesn't do anyone any good. Since we know we've fallen and will continue to fall, the question isn't "How can I stop myself from falling ever again?" Instead, it's "*When* I fall, what am I going to do next?" Having safe-

---

25 Paul Hawson, personal interview, 2015.

guards in our life like specific verses and people to be accountable to so that we fall less is a great place when we're being tempted and after we fall into temptation. Whether we choose to seek to be further restored in a godly fashion is completely up to us. We can focus inwardly on ourselves or decide to fix our eyes on the lavish, unmerited grace we're given over and over again. In the ongoing journey of sanctification, there will be bumps and stumbles along the road but when we choose to lean on God, we can rise from the ground and get back on the horse again.

Jesus,

Despite what the Enemy may make us believe, You aren't pointing Your finger at us in scorn every time we fall or mess up. Give us strength to go to You so the common pitfalls in our lives become less and less common.

In Jesus' Name, Amen.

DAY 53

FINANCIALLY FAITHFUL

1 Timothy 6:10

Regardless of your financial background, Jesus' words about not storing up treasure on Earth are still true and applicable. Money itself is not an evil, mustache-twirling monstrosity. We can use our money for many worthwhile things that honor Christ. Money can be used to fund a mission trip to those who may never hear about Jesus otherwise. Money can be used to buy a plane ticket so you can visit a grieving relative who just lost their spouse. Money can be used to pay for someone else's meal to show them the love of God. The problem is when we see it as anything other than a tool to further God's Kingdom. That being said, college is a prime time to learn financial habits that will glorify God and help others going forward. Asking older, trusted believers who've dealt with handling money as an adult can be very helpful. It's important to be good stewards of however much God has entrusted us with, whether that's your resources, talents, or anything else. I am by no means an expert in monetary management but either extreme on the spectrum like frivolous spending or hoarding isn't the attitude we are to have towards money. What matters most is realizing that nothing we own is ours and that it doesn't matter how big of a check we sign if our heart's not with Him.

Lord,

Forgive us for seeing what You've graciously given us and responding with, "Mine!" Please give us wisdom and humility in how to use the financial resources or any resource You've given us for Your honor and glory.

In Jesus' Name, Amen.

TASTE AND SEE

Psalm 34:8

The Dark Knight[26] is one of the most raved- and talk-ed-about movies of all time and rightfully so. The complicated themes of morality and justice, Hans Zimmer's breathtaking score, and of course, Heath Ledger's masterful performance of Joker leave many positive things to talk about regarding the film. For years, I've talked about how great it is and have recommended it to others. They become shocked when I reveal that I've never actually watched the movie from beginning to end (and I still haven't gotten around to doing so). My testimony about how good it is becomes less trustworthy because I've never actually seen or experienced it myself, I've only shared what I heard about it.

Oftentimes as Christians, we can be the same way. We can talk about how good God is without truly knowing what doing life with Christ looks like. If we're not actively seek-

---

26 *The Dark Knight*. Directed by Christopher Nolan, performances by
    Christian Bale, Heath Ledger, Gary Oldman, and Michael Caine,
    Warner Bros. Pictures, 2008.

ing a deeper relationship with Him, other people aren't just missing out because they're being stubborn. They're missing out because they see we're missing out as they don't see us truly enjoying a God-centered life. As a result, they're skeptical of how fulfilling, awesome, and majestic our God is. We don't have to just hear from other believers how awesome Jesus is. We can trust hearing that because we could already be sitting at His feet. You can't pour out of any empty cup, and allowing ourselves to be filled with His all-consuming love enables us to tell others the goodness of God better because that's a daily reality for us.

Father,

We can talk a big game about how awesome You are without that talk being reflected in how we live. Show us the discrepancies in what we claim to believe versus what our lives look like so others are not led astray.

In Jesus' Name, Amen.

DAY 55

TOUGH LOVE IS TOUGH

2 Timothy 1:7

After Israel messed up again (surprise, surprise), God allowed the countries around them to attack them again and again as if they were a small child knocked down by a crashing wave. Being the merciful God He is, He answered Israel's cry for help in the form of Gideon, who is, in my opinion, one of the most relatable people in biblical history. When an angel gives him his mission on God's behalf, his immediate response is one of fear and doubt, questioning God's presence in the difficult situation the Israelites found themselves in. He states that in the puniest tribe of Israel, he is at the bottom of the food chain being the youngest. Eventually, Gideon gets down to it after God confirms Himself with a sign or two but even in his obedience, he's still shaking at his knees. It's amazing, though, that God doesn't ask for more strength than we have. He's not angry at whatever amount of strength and faith we can give, but patiently says, "That's okay. I can work with that." Sometimes, the initial encouragement about Him never leaving or forsaking His children eases us until we're in the process of having to trust and rely on Him. It's easy to feel like we're not battle-ready because of how fearful we can be. If we're being honest, when we look in the mirror, most of us see a scared little kid who's in way over his/her head. Our God doesn't see what we see in ourselves, though. The first thing the angel said to Gideon was "Mighty hero." That's how God sees us when we're scared because He's good at turning us into what we're not.

Abba,

We're often scared even when we're doing what You ask of us. Help us do whatever it is anyway, trusting You give us ample reason to be courageous.

In Jesus' Name, Amen.

TAKE A RISK

Isaiah 43:19

It's an amazing paradox that we jump at the thought of something new happening in our lives but are too afraid of the unknown to try it. I know the prospect of something new excites and terrifies me because while I always appreciate a nice change of pace, I can grow used to and comfortable with what's always been, even if it's not growing me. We certainly need to remember the past and God's faithfulness then, but may we never live in the past and not see what God is doing in our midst now. If we do see it, may we not decide to not participate in His plan out of a misguided sense of accomplishment as we've already "done our part" serving God. The thing is, our God is not a "once-and-done" God. He's a living and active Creator who doesn't take a day off from His plans and neither should we. Rest, of course, is essential, but we're missing out big time if we don't see the things He's doing in the present. I know how hard it is to imagine something new when the dreaded same-old sticks around for a while. His new thing for you could be taking a job that doesn't pay much but brings a new challenge that will grow you. His new thing for you could be a community you're not super well-acquainted with. His new thing could even just be switching up your quiet time to keep the intimacy fresh, like reading one book of the Bible consistently or starting your time in the Word with silence. Whatever it is, I urge you to grab onto the adventure and see where it takes you.

Jesus,

You offer radical transformation and regular renewal in our lives, which inherently means something has to change. Help us go where You lead us and leave the comfort and say "Yes" to the adventure of doing life with You.

In Your Name, Amen.

IT'S TIME TO SURRENDER

Romans 12:1-2

The word "surrender" can make a lot of us quiver, as it implies giving up something or yourself and someone else having victory over you. It can be more daunting when we realize the processes of submission and transformation are supposed to be commonplace in our walks with God, not just when we first come to faith. If I'm being honest, there are many times when I just want to do what I feel is right for myself and not have to give my choices up, not to others and especially not to God. My pride makes me think I know best and God's just an overbearing tyrant. That is, before reality comes back in and I'm shown just how helpless I am apart from God. Surrendering your comforts, bad habits, and other things is hard. What God wants most from us is our hearts. Our lives. Our *everything*. Jesus knew how hard this was. Right before his crucifixion, He begged God to take away the agony He would feel on behalf of humanity. Yet even to the point of sweating blood, He proclaimed, "Not

My will but Your will be done." We talk about our rights, but Jesus, who had and still has the rights, willingly gave them up so anyone, no matter what they've done, could come to Him and be saved. When we realize the depths of His surrender and how much better life is with Him calling the shots, we can experience the transformation that comes with giving up our lives for Him and others.

God,

Surrender is not comfortable, but it's the way of Jesus, and it should be a daily thing as Your followers. Transform us into the people You're making us into, and help us let go of what's keeping us from being those people.

In Jesus' Name, Amen.

ONE ARMY, DIFFERENT INFANTRY ROLES

Galatians 3:28

In both the Old and the New Testaments, the average Jew did not hold a particularly high opinion of a Gentile. To them, a Gentile was what we would nowadays call "a bum." Unclean. Unworthy. *That* person. God did tell the Israelites to steer clear of marrying people from other nations in the Old Testament, but it had nothing to do with their skin color or ethnicity. It had everything to do with their sinful practices and idol worship. That being said, Jesus made it explicitly clear that the "Jew's Jew" wasn't getting saved unless he put his trust in Christ. Enter Paul, who matched that description to a tee and states in Philippians 3 that because of what Christ has done, his good deeds are worthless in comparison. We meet all sorts of different folk from different walks of life in college, and I'm not even talking about unbelievers or people of other faiths. It's so easy to categorize people who do things differently than we might or think it's impossible to associate with them based on how "out there" they are. What's so wonderful is the love of Christ made it so that Simon the Zealot, a Jewish revolutionary looking to overthrow the Romans, and Matthew, a Jewish traitor working for them, could call each other "brother." We are all looking for acceptance and to be a part of something bigger than ourselves, but for those in God's Kingdom, everyone is truly, objectively equal. We all have a vital part to play. If someone who says they love Jesus claims superiority over you, remind them that a true Christian influencer with millions of followers on TikTok is on the same playing field as a genuine disciple saying, "My pleasure" from behind the cash register.

Holy Spirit,

We praise You for breaking the wall of hostility not just between us and You but our neighbors and the people we see on a daily basis. Break any division among other believers in our lives and help us see everyone as someone Christ thought was worth dying for.

In Jesus' Name, Amen.

CONTEXT IS KEY

Colossians 3:5

Contrary to what some people within the church would lead you to think, the God of the universe doesn't think sex is dirty at all. Why would He? After all, He designed it. It's meant to be a special form of intimacy between a man and woman in marriage. When it's in that context, it's not just permissible but beautiful. It just becomes a problem when it is taken out of these parameters that God laid out for it. The struggle to wait until marriage can be hard when our peers can view it in a far more casual way than we do as believers. Our culture has taken sexuality and tried to bend it and twist it to what they feel it should be rather than how God intended it to be. Even if we do the right thing and wait for marriage, it can be a struggle to not look at someone you don't know in a degrading way when you're scrolling on your laptop or phone at night. God wants us to enjoy sex if that's our desire but to truly enjoy it, we need to take it as He intended, no more, no less. Additionally, far more than sex, far more than a pure and loving relationship with the other person, He wants us to enjoy Him most. Satan's attempts to tempt us to commit sexual immorality in any form are tactical, as we're the next generation and our patterns in this area could either work in his favor or detriment. Being plain to God is so important, but having people to be accountable to invites others to lift us up when we fall sexually. Death is always painful, but with the Spirit's help, we can find freedom from this specific pit Satan tries to keep us in.

Lord,

This is a hard area that we often brush aside because it's painful to address. Help us be vulnerable knowing Your mercy and grace is on the other side of repenting from any sexual sin in our lives.

In Jesus' Name, Amen.

IT'S OKAY TO LOOK WEIRD

Psalm 33:8

If there's one name in the animal world in Earth's history that demands respect, it's Tyrannosaurus *Rex*. Its name means "tyrant lizard king." Measuring longer than forty feet and easily weighing over nine tons on average, it was the most physically dominant land predator to ever live. Unlike other carnivores whose teeth were designed for slicing and dicing flesh, their teeth are comparable to railroad spikes and could close their bone-crushing jaws with enough force to absolutely *flatten* a car. They had eyes rivaling a hawk and a sense of smell that surpassed a bloodhound. They were also quite brainy for a predator their size. Contrary to popular belief, rather than a thunderous roar, if they wanted to make their presence known, scientists believe they would emit a low rumble that would make your spine quiver. All of these attributes make *T-Rex* earn its title as definite "King of the Dinosaurs."

If a magnificent animal like this is deserving to be admired, how much more worthy is our God to be awed and worshipped? A dangerous thing can come after we're saved, where we grow "used" to Him and take Him for granted. The childlike excitement of being His child can fade, and we forget to give God the praise and reverence He's due for who He is and what He's done for us. He's our personal, eternal Abba, but let us never forget to approach Him with total and naked awe.

Almighty God,

Your awe-inspiring character and deeds should always make us stop and simply worship. We praise You because You are deserving of it and because it reminds us that we're Your children who are ever-dependent on You.

In Jesus' Name, Amen.

JUSTICE IS SERVED

Isaiah 1:17

There seems to be a high demand for justice, especially in our age demographic. Many would like to portray Jesus as their own social justice warrior who came specifically to fight for their identified political ideology. He didn't: His main goal was to come to seek and save the lost. That being said, Jesus *does* have clear standards about how we are to treat the poor and marginalized. In the second chapter of James, it's made crystal clear that it's kind of pointless to wish a brother or sister in Christ warmth when you're wearing a fabric that could grant them that very thing but don't offer it. All of us were on the outskirts and destitute in our sin, and the fact that He bothered to not only look in our direction but do something about our state of being should inspire us to help those who are often overlooked. I'm not saying to empty your bank account, as that's not what Jesus asks of you. The only time He asked that of someone was to make a point that the rich person asking to follow Him was boasting in his good deeds rather than in Him. Motivation for speaking up for the rights of others is key, and integrity means doing the right thing when no one's looking or going on a mission trip without feeling the need to post about it to be admired on Instagram. There are plenty of opportunities to serve around you, and it's a prime time to take responsibility by asking the question, "If not me, who?"

God,

You didn't give us eyes and ears so we would turn a blind eye or a deaf ear to those who desperately need to feel seen or loved. Show us where we can be Your hands and feet and give Your love freely as we've been freely given.

In Jesus' Name, Amen.

DAY 62

THE COMMON DENOMINATOR

Romans 3:23

Everyone makes mistakes. *Everyone*. We have been sinful since we've been in our mother's womb, and we'll continue to sin until we pass onto the other side of eternity. Jesus came down to pay the penalty for our sins so we could have forgiveness from them. We're humbled when we realize forgiveness can only be given to a sinner, which is what Jesus and the Bible call us. I'll be frank: I don't really like that diagnosis. The fact that I don't like it doesn't mean it's not right on the money, though. Many religious leaders during Christ's time were too self-righteous to admit the sin sickness that plagued mankind was just as much their problem as it was for corrupt tax collectors or prostitutes. If a doctor tells a patient they have a life-threatening illness and that there is a cure for it, do you think the patient is going to linger on the fact they're not healthy or focus on the thing that can make them better? When we tell people about Jesus' death and resurrection, we would be doing them a massive disservice by not telling them *why* he had to die: to punish sin as God is just and to set us free as God is loving. It's not our job to convict; it's the Holy Spirit's, but unless we tell people about the thing He saved us from, why would they ever think they need a Savior in the first place? Knowing we all sin can also help us not put people on a pedestal or make them caricatures, as they need to be redeemed every bit as we need to. Recognizing how broken we are is painful but makes our perception of God more glorious that He loves us in a way we cannot wrap our mind around.

King Jesus,

Thank You for loving us despite all we do, and for drawing us close to You. Grant us the humility to realize that the only thing we contributed to our salvation was the sin we needed to be saved from.

In Jesus' Name, Amen.

DAY 63

SPIRITUAL GUARDRAILS

Ephesians 6:10-18

In *Apocalypse Now*,[27] Captain Willard is sanctioned by his higher-ups to go deep into the jungles of 'Nam and end the life of Colonel Kurtz, a soldier gone rogue who is far beyond his breaking point. Willard soon finds that the deeper he and his crew go into the river, the more abstract concepts like "humanity" and "sanity" become as the chaos and darkness surround them at increasing levels. After finally meeting the crazed colonel, it becomes clear to Willard that Kurtz's twisted philosophy stems from a recognition that there is an unseen enemy beyond the localized fighting taking place in that pit and that enemy is the capacity that lies within each human heart for rage, murder, and lust.

As Christians, we, too, have an enemy who works from behind the scenes beneath the notice of the average person. The evil one's sole focus is on the total destruction of any-

---

27 *Apocalypse Now*. Directed by Francis Ford Coppola, performances by Martin Sheen, Marlon Brando, Robert Duvall, and Laurence Fishburne, Omni Zoetrope, 1979.

one or anything resembling Jesus. We are soldiers with a supreme commander and are still to fight this battle no matter what it costs us. I'm not trying to intimidate you, but I want to make you aware of the spiritual goings-on in our world. It's important to know that while there is still conflict, the war itself is over and the clear victor is seen in Christ. On top of that, we're given armor that rivals Tony Stark's and allows us to go on the offensive and defensive. So let's put on our spiritual protective clothing daily and opt to take part in this war knowing it's already been won by Jesus.

God,

We've graciously been allowed to share Your victory over sin and death, but that doesn't mean there is no more fighting to do. Arm us with Your tools so we can not only stand our ground but gain ground for Your Kingdom.

In Jesus' Name, Amen.

CREATION IS BREATHTAKING. GOD IS MORE SO.

Psalm 19:1

If you ever need to be reminded how much God loves you, just go on a walk and see His creation on full display. In this verse, David gives credit where credit is due about whose radiance is reflected in the design of the cosmos. He makes it a point to describe God's magnificent creation as "His glory" because that is literally the only way to describe it. To be honest, the immense glory of the Lord has made me afraid to draw near to Him in the past. I thought that the God who keeps the hydrogen in the many, many, *many* stars in the galaxy in order would think talking to a speck like me was beneath Him. Being on the spectrum, my mind doesn't jive well with intangibles and my doubts about Him made me think He got everything else in creation right but me. After all, why would He want to talk to someone who doesn't believe, think, or go through life in a way that's "normal"? It wasn't until I read the second description, "His handiwork," that I realized He wasn't some distant cosmic battery but that He created everything with intentionality and an intimate personal touch only a loving Father could have. If He perfectly keeps track of trillions of things that need to happen to keep the universe running, then that means He knew what He was doing making me and everyone else. Trees aren't particularly chatty. The pebbles aren't one to give congressional addresses. That doesn't mean that they and everything in nature don't say the same thing every day constantly: God knows and loves His image-bearers and deeply longs for them to know and love Him back.

Almighty Creator,

So often, we're guilty of not stopping to smell the roses and truly appreciate Your fingerprints on everything we see. Thank You for nature, a divine symphony pointing back to You.

In Jesus' Name, Amen.

HE GIVES GRACE

Jeremiah 31:3

If I were in God's shoes, I would have given up on Israel a long time ago. Time after time, they're given chances to repent and come back to His tender care, and a lot of times they do just that only to spit in the face of God and chase inferior alternatives. The thing is, in this time period when your family or culture worshiped a certain god, you stuck with that god, regardless of whether it was true or not, and turning your back on the god you knew was considered bad form. To do that would be a level of insanity that even pagans, people who worshiped false idols and counterfeit deities, would never *ever* do. That is probably one reason God commanded the Israelites to destroy other nations because the likelihood of them going to the one true God was minuscule, to say the least. The Israelites were God's chosen people, but they had a habit of treating that like it was nothing. I know I rarely appreciate the depths of God's love for me and when I stray, I'm hesitant to go back as if God was as unforgiving as I can be. When I muster up the courage to go back to Him after I mess up, do you know what I get? Steadfast love. Tender mercy. Boundless compassion. Things I know I don't deserve. God's not looking at you like a problem but a child. He is totally head over heels in love with you and can't contain His joy when He thinks of being with you. The more we remind ourselves of His kindness, the more we'll *want* to stay close to Him because although we weren't needed, He *wanted* us.

Father,

You're better and kinder to us than we could ever deserve, and we praise You for that. Help us trust that Your grace is unending because of who You are, not because of what we have done.

In Jesus's Name, Amen.

SLOW YOUR ROLL

Mark 10:45

A phenomenon called "hustle culture" where productivity and success are the zenith of everything has so many people (especially those our age) hooked on its appeal until they're drained of the mental, spiritual, and physical strength to go on. As is typical in our culture, studies examining this lifestyle tend to focus on the harm it causes the collective "I" and tend to skip over the harm we can cause others to face. The allure of hustle culture tends to make one forget that in order to climb up its hierarchy, you often need to step over other people to achieve your goals. People can be so afraid of being forgotten or wanting to be great that it doesn't matter who gets hurt as long as their "me, myself, and I" is served. Being the sons of a fisherman in an economy where that was integral to society, James and John thought they could transfer how to be great as a businessman to being great in the Kingdom. They took His lessons of "ask and it will be given to you" to heart by asking Him to make them great. As was typical of Jesus, he went against the culture and what it considered "great." Jesus showed them and the rest of the disciples that true great-ness in God's Kingdom is, as Steve Rogers said, "to lay down on a wire and let the other guy crawl over you."[28] It means washing the feet of the men who will betray you to the op-pressive government and who will deny you not once, not twice, but thrice. It means dying a humiliating and unde-served death and giving access to salvation to those who want nothing to do with you. Let's remind ourselves that being high on the totem pole in the Kingdom means get-ting acquainted with the dirt below the wooden post.

Lord,

Forgive us for grabbing for power and seeing what we've been given as our own rather than things to steward faithfully in the service of others. Grant us humility to have the mindset of You first, others second, and ourselves last in all we do.

In Jesus' Name, Amen.

---

28 *The Avengers*. Directed by Joss Whedon, performances by Robert Downey Jr., Tom Hiddleston, Chris Evans, and Mark Ruffalo, Walt Disney Studios Motion Pictures, 2012.

BE HONEST IN YOUR DOUBTS

John 20:29

Thomas gets a lot of undeserved flack among the original twelve disciples. The dude left everything behind to faithfully follow Jesus like all the other disciples, but he's always remembered as "Doubting Thomas" just because he has standards of evidence. Honestly, if I were in his shoes, I would have doubted and not just jumped to the "radical" possibility that Jesus proved He was who He said He was. When his brothers came to him frantically and excitedly proclaiming their Lord has risen, he said he wouldn't believe until he had been plainly laid out the conditions that would compel him to. A little bit later, Jesus met all of Thomas's criteria for believing and our guy returned to form. Jesus' response is that those who don't have these supernatural experiences yet trust in Him are richly blessed. That always struck me as illogical because as someone with autism, blind belief doesn't always roll with me. I'm often twiddling my thumbs waiting for God to do a miraculous thing because despite seeing Him move amazingly in the past, the feelings of doubt creep in and can influence my thinking to believe they were flukes. It's comforting that God's desire for us to believe in Him isn't a fairytale but based on truth and reality. It helps to learn some basic apologetics about God, the resurrection, and miracles, and I definitely recommend learning the historical facts about Jesus. That being said, knowing a lot of facts about someone doesn't mean you know them as a person. Tyler Staton notes in *Searching for Enough: The High Wire Walk Between Faith and Doubt*[29] that the Hebrew word "*yada*" means to know in an intimate way, contrary to the belief that knowledge is just facts and belief is deeper. The facts of the resurrection draw us in more than fuzzy feelings. We're invited every day to bring our doubts and questions to God and call Him what He really is, "My Lord and my God."

Lord,

We realize that the discrepancy between the finiteness of our human mind and the vastness of Your eternal person can create feelings of doubt that can be quite scary. Thank You for Your reassurance that we can bring our questions to You and work it out with You.

In Jesus' Name, Amen.

---

29 Tyler Staton, *Searching for Enough: The High-Wire Walk Between Faith and Doubt* (Zondervan, 2021).

LISTEN AND HEAR TO SEE AND LOVE

James 1:19

When engaging with people of different beliefs, apologist Sean McDowell recommends that before we seek to be *understood*, we must seek to *understand*.[30] This principle doesn't just apply when talking to unbelievers but to anyone. People our age want to be understood and seen, but we are unwilling to extend that courtesy to others. If I'm being honest, I care more about being heard than hearing someone else most of the time. I know in the past I've tried to overstep and do the job that only the Holy Spirit can do of convincing and convicting. In other cases of listening, when someone is going through something really hard, we can genuinely have the best of intentions and try to fix their problems or offer a solution. That's not to say that isn't helpful, but most of us don't want a PowerPoint presentation when we open up: we want the gift of being

---

30 Sean McDowell and Tim Muehlhoff, *End the Stalemate: Move Past Cancel Culture to Meaningful Conversations* (Tyndale Elevate, 2024).

present and with open ears. Even something as daunting as putting social media scrolling on hold for a few minutes to allow someone else to take you up on your offer of "How was your day?" Listening is a hard skill to master when whomever we're speaking with is frustrating us or our attention is elsewhere. The thing we have to remember, though, is that while Jesus certainly rebuked those who claimed heresy against Him, He never prevented them from saying their two cents, even though He disagreed heavily with them. He gave this simple gift to the lowest of the low after years of thinking they would never be able to tell others how they felt. In the many of the healings He did, He stopped whatever He was doing prior and listened to the person's story before the miraculous occurred. I'm certainly still learning in this area, as a lot of my "listening" has been nodding my head just so I could say my piece after. The challenge of listening with no strings attached is hard, but it becomes less daunting when we realize our God is a God who is always willing to listen to us.

God,

Thank You for listening to our cries, praises, questions, and anything we feel is worth being listened to. Help us emulate Your listening nature so others can feel safe to talk to us and feel seen and loved.

In Jesus' Name, Amen.

DOWN TO THE BASICS

Matthew 22:37-38

We were created for God and for each other. When asked by an expert in the law what the most important law was, Jesus answered it's to love God with everything in you and a close second, to love your neighbor as yourself. Irreligious people can respect the love Christians show to each other and others while thinking the former is unnecessary for doing the latter. That's simply not the case, though. If we don't love God the most in our lives, our priorities, no matter how well-intentioned, will always be misplaced. Our love for others would eventually turn into an attempt to make them the God of our hearts and minds. We would then just be using them to fill the empty hole in our lives. We lose perspective as to why it's best to love others if we only exist to be nice to others with no greater purpose such as loving God. Take it from a perpetual people pleaser, that's not as noble as it sounds and definitely not healthy in any sense. God created us for Him to be our number one because that's what our soul needs and that's what He deserves to be in our lives. When we keep the main thing the main thing, we're learning from the Master how to love others while learning to love Him most.

God,

You want us to make You our absolute everything and when we do that, others are best loved. We pray for strength to set boundaries that keep You the priority in our relationships so Your will might be done.

In Jesus' Name, Amen.

A RETOLD STORY

Isaiah 43:1

Of all the redemption arcs that have been depicted in media, none is perhaps as noteworthy or just plain *good* as the one of Prince Zuko in *Avatar: The Last Airbender*,[31] an animated television show. The heir to the Fire Nation desires his place on the throne and his honor to be restored after he's banished by his "father" while on a wild goose chase to find the Avatar who has been missing for over a century. What separates him from other arcs is that throughout his whole journey, he stumbles and makes mistakes in a way that's not static but dynamic and relatable for the viewer. He eventually sees the Fire Nation, one of the four nations of the world he lives in, and its deals and his father are not what he wants but love and acceptance. Eventually, he joins up with his former enemies and becomes an integral part of stopping his father and saving the world. As satisfying as it is seeing his redemption, the fact is no one can redeem the mess they put themselves in on their own. There were

---

31 Daniel Michael DiMartino and Bryan Konietzko, creators, *Avatar: The Last Airbender*, Nickelodeon Animation Studio, 2005–2008.

many systems of sacrifice that God enacted for His people Israel, but whether by ignoring them completely or adding extra rules, Israel missed the mark and tried as they might, and they drifted further and farther from their Shepherd, unable to course-correct back to God as much as they tried.

In many ways, Israel in the Old Testament is us. We sin and turn our backs on God again and again, and we can't make ourselves right with Him on our own, even if we want to. When we get into this mindset, we hold ourselves and others on a legalistic pedestal and have the same mindset as the people Jesus frequently rebuked. God wasn't satisfied with us not knowing Him so He bought us back at an enormous cost. He did that because you're His. You don't need to do "X, Y, or even Z," to obtain it. Just ask and then abide in Him.

Jesus,

The redemption that was bought came at a heavy price, but You still went through with it because Your love is incomprehensibly huge. Help us go about our days with confidence in our freedom and humility in that it was achieved solely by You.

In Jesus' Name, Amen.

A FRESH START

Micah 7:18-20

Billionaire. Genius. Philanthropist. These are just a few words that describe Tony Stark, and boy, did he bask in each one as the world's premier weapon designer. Ironically, it wasn't until he almost lost his heart in a terrorist attack that he got his own cardiovascular organ. He saw firsthand that the tech he had designed to protect young troops was being used against them. With the help of another captive, Dr. Yinsen, he escapes in armor he made in a cave from a box of scraps. After Yinsen gives up his life to buy Stark enough time to escape, the cocky genius is humbled and thanks him for saving his life. With his dying breath, the good doctor advises, "Don't waste your life." Though Tony Stark made a lot of mistakes along the way, he made the most of his second chance at life by shutting down his company's weapon division and protecting the world in an ever-evolving suit of armor as Iron Man.[32]

---

32 *Iron Man*. Directed by Jon Favreau, performances by Robert Downey Jr., Jeff Bridges, Gwyneth Paltrow, and Terrence Howard, Marvel Studios, 2008.

Everyone wants a second chance after falling hard. However, humanity couldn't just shake the dust off its feet and strive to "do better." We all were in a pit of our own making with no pulse and no hope of getting out. That was until Christ brought us out of it, giving us an opportunity to see what real living looks like. So many Christians can treat their salvation as "hell insurance" rather than something to work out with fear and trembling as Paul says. If it's truly our greatest hope, then we should strive to act on it in all we do. Jesus made it possible by bearing our punishment, and now, we can bear witness as He pulverizes everything that holds us back from going all in for Him. He's thrown your completely forgiven sin into the deepest depths, so with His grace, you can soar to the highest heights as you serve Him.

Lord,

You died so that from now on we would live for You. You redeemed us at a tremendous cost. May we never take for granted the life we get to live through the power of Your Holy Spirit.

In Jesus' Name, Amen.

REMEMBER, KIDS

Psalm 139:13-14

You may or may not have heard it from a tomato named Bob, but I'll clue you in just in case: God made you special and loves you *very* much. The same applies to everyone you see or meet. There was no plan "B" about how the dude doing work on his laptop in the commons was supposed to look. There wasn't an alternate way God intended for the dude putting food in grocery bags to appear. Sin did corrupt His creation, but it doesn't change the fact that everyone is made exactly as they're supposed to be. He knows us infinitely better than we could ever know ourselves. That doesn't mean we don't occasionally put on an art critic's hat and judge His design on us as if He's an aspiring artist who needs our validation to see His workmanship as good. News flash: He doesn't need our approval on *anything*. Because He's God and can only be good and perfect, that translates to mean that whatever He makes is only good and perfect. Unfortunately, that truth can be lost in your mind and heart when you feel as though you're broken or don't "work." Being autistic and having OCD is one of God's personal, loving handprints in my life; that didn't stop me from resenting that I would have to deal with the ramifications of living with both for the rest of my life. For years, I felt like an outsider even after taking my faith seriously and trying to consistently surround myself with other teenagers striving to follow Jesus better. No one intentionally excluded me, but I still felt like I was just *there*. Maybe you have felt like your body doesn't look like it should. It could be that you have similar struggles with neurodivergence. It's entirely possible there's something about His design in you that *really* grinds your gears in a totally different way. Regardless, we need to remember that our God is not in the business of making junk. You are not junk. God promises us in Romans 8 that we'll have new bodies that resemble Him but, until then, give thanks for the fact that how He made you is pretty dang fantastic.

Lord,

Every hair, skin cell, and feature of our bodies are hand-crafted and put there for a reason. Give us eyes to see ourselves the way You do and praise You for what a creative and loving God You are.

In Jesus' Name, Amen.

KEEP THE LINE CLEAR

1 Corinthians 10:31

When we consider a course of action, we might find ourselves asking, "Is it a sin?" If the answer is "no," we press on to the activity as if we knew our course of action all along and just wanted to do it without feeling guilty. In the polytheistic culture of Paul's time, it was common to offer meat to idols, and obviously, the Corinthian believers knew it was no question they had to abandon their counterfeit gods in light of this new relationship with Jesus. The more nuanced question they asked is, "How do we navigate the freedom we have in Christ and avoid legalism while at the same time maintaining holiness in our day-to-day lives?" This question came in the context of whether or not it was ok to eat meat in the marketplace they once used in their idol worship. Some thought it was not an extraordinarily big deal and that meat was meat, while others felt that eating the meat was still sinful and in violation of what God wanted for them. Paul's point was that regardless of your own personal conviction, using your freedom in Him means being mindful of not using it to cause others to stumble.

Jesus had certain words in Matthew 18 about those who cause little ones in the faith to stumble, and they weren't particularly pleasant. In order to avoid making someone else trip up, that may mean we may have to give up some of our choices—if giving up those choices means someone else's spiritual growth won't be inhibited. That can be a tough pill to swallow, but our freedom should never be used to flaunt but to build up others. Additionally, thinking in the absolute broadest sense, this verse should be every believer's aspiration for their life. When we stop asking, "Is this a sin?" and start asking, "Does this glorify God?" then our standard of living gets raised. It's hard, but if we're just seeking what's permissible rather than what will honor Jesus, we're missing out on what really living set apart for Him looks like. We have so much liberty, but let's not abuse that knowing our fellow brothers and sisters are closely watching how we praise God in our daily decisions.

Father,

It is for freedom that Christ has set us free but that freedom shouldn't be taken for granted. Help us live the lives we were always intended to live and do everything for Your honor and glory.

In Jesus' Name, Amen.

THE CARDS YOU'RE DEALT

Jeremiah 29:11

In *Rise of the Guardians*,[33] Jack Frost wakes from a frozen lake and discovers he possesses the ability to fly and manipulate ice, powers given to him by the Man on the Moon. These incredible gifts are significantly dulled when he finds he has no memory of his past life. On top of that, he's not able to simply start from scratch and make new connections because people are unable to see, hear, or touch him, essentially making him a phantom for *three hundred years*. Resentment and confusion builds up as he spends many a night angrily accusing the Man of the Moon of robbing him of something amazing—and he doesn't even know what he was being robbed of. He begins to question why he's even here and what his purpose is.

---

33 *Rise of the Guardians*. Directed by Peter Ramsey, performances by Chris Pine, Alec Baldwin, Hugh Jackman, and Jude Law, Paramount Pictures, 2012.

We, too, can question the components of God's plan in our life. Of course, God does have a plan and can only plan that which is good because He is good, but that doesn't mean every little thing involved in His plan seems good in the moment. After being politely escorted (or conquered and forcibly driven out, who's to say?) by Babylon, the Israelites wanted some encouraging word from God in their exile. He told them they would regain their land in, give or take, seventy years. A real pick-me-up. This verse doesn't promise everything will always be sunshine and rainbows. What it promises is that even if something is out of our control or bad, we can find comfort in His trustworthiness. Nothing we go through lacks purpose. We just have to see it as a chance for us to be changed to become more like Him. God's ultimate endgame for His people that's undeterred in all circumstances can be described the same way He describes us in Genesis: very good.

Lord,

The things we deal with are hard and we don't understand them. Help us be patient, and help us see that every hard thing that comes our way isn't unknown to You and is a chance to be formed more and more into the image of Your Son.

In Jesus' Name, Amen.

THE JUNK FROM WITHIN

Galatians 5:17

In almost every iteration of the Spider-Man lore, the Wall Crawler finds himself coming in contact with an alien symbiote. The extraterrestrial symbiote hails from the cosmos and like the rest of its kind, needs a host to latch onto in order to feast on their neurochemicals. One symbiote finds its way onto Spider-Man when he's on an adventure with his superhero allies. The symbiote enhances the friendly neighborhood's already exceptional physical abilities and his crime-fighting game gets a massive upgrade. There are no drawbacks initially. The symbiote, however, amplifies its host's aggression and inherent flaws to a degree that is dangerous to everyone around it. Spider-Man's natural sense of justice and self-deprecating humor don't change into vengeful wrath and bitter self-loathing out of nowhere. They were always there, lurking within the dark parts of Parker. It's simply easier to see because of the symbiote. To rid himself of it, he bangs the black suit against a clock, as the symbiote is hypersensitive to vibrations.[34]

---

34 *Spider-Man 3*. Directed by Sam Raimi, performances by Tobey Maguire, Kirsten Dunst, James Franco, and J. K. Simmons, Columbia Pictures, 2007.

Unfortunately for us, if we try to rid ourselves of our flesh by banging against a big metal clock, we'll still have our sin, just in a broken frame. We are fully forgiven and are new creations with new desires to seek God, but the war between the two realms outside of our bodies starts to take place within ourselves in the form of our flesh and spirit. Paul says the flesh and Spirit are in a constant tug of war for control and *really* don't like each other (Galatians 5:17). Each choice we make will cause one of them to squirm. We'll always face temptations, and we'll never *always* want to live for Him on this side of glory. The solution isn't to legalistically strive to do it on your resources. It's to abide by the life-giving Advocate Jesus promised we would have when we accepted His invitation to His Kingdom. We still have a part to play, though, in regards to removing stuff in our lives that makes the flesh a happy camper. We're going to lose some fights against temptations, but God's Spirit who raised Jesus from the dead can help us gather more wins than losses.

Holy Spirit,

Death is a daily part of our life as followers of Jesus but after death in Your Kingdom, there is always resurrection. Thank You that we're not doing this battle alone, and we have You, our brothers and sisters in Christ, and Your Word to comfort and encourage us.

In Jesus' Name, Amen.

UNLIKELY ASSETS

2 Corinthians 12:9-10

Have you ever noticed that when God calls someone to do something for Him in the Bible, it's oftentimes *not* the person with the best credentials or the one most likely destined for greatness in the eyes of others? He has a certain way of making those others call "nothing" into something great and those who call themselves great into nothing. In an underrated story of the Bible, Israel cried to God for help after messing up for the umpteenth time. The Lord sent a man called Ehud to permanently end the king of Moab's reign. To do that, he needed to catch the pagan king off guard and make himself seem as though he was not a threat so he could get in close enough. Fortunately for the judge, he was left-handed, the opposite of most would-be assassins at the time, and, therefore, the least likely person to try to kill the king. After getting alone with the king, he says he has a message from God in a way that resembles many pre-kill one-liners today before plunging his dagger deep into the king's hide and freeing his people (Judges 3:15-30). Our perceived limitations don't speak less

THE RIGHT ROCK: 100 DAY DEVOTIONAL

about God using us but more as we see He's a chess master who can turn things that, by themselves, are not strengths into strengths. Our God is in the business of using whatever weakness we and others think serves no purpose for our good and His glory.

Jesus,

You make all things new, and that includes making the limitations about us the biggest assets we can offer to further Your Kingdom. We surrender anything we may believe to be holding us back and ask that You use it in ways we haven't even considered.

In Jesus' Name, Amen.

DELAYING THE INEVITABLE

Hebrews 10:39

High-speed chases are certainly suspenseful, even exhilarating, and can be the source of much frustration regarding how much longer the chase should be and how we could do the boys in blue's job better than them if we were in the cop cruiser. That doesn't change the fact that the outcome is always known from the start. The person gets caught and we all leave satisfied that justice was served. I think if I could talk to a high-speed suspect, I would be tempted to ask, "Did you *really* think you were getting away?" As less of an answer as a would-be getaway driver would have for that question, Jonah's response would have been even less so considering he tried to make himself scarce from almighty God (Jonah 1:3). After God asked him to go and preach repentance to Nineveh, Jonah decided to do a "pro-gamer move" in his mind and disobeyed the calling God gave him. He went in the exact opposite direction God asked him to go aboard a Gentile ship. The Lord formed a storm to get

Jonah's attention, which endangered the crew, showing him and us that the consequences of disobedience don't just hurt the disobedient person but the people around us.

Dying to ourselves daily and obeying His will over ours doesn't come naturally to us. I know it doesn't for me. When we're running *away* from God, where do we think we're running *to*? Something better than the joy and purpose that comes from obeying Jesus? If we turn our backs on Him, we miss out on that, not to mention the impact we could have on someone else's life. It's never too late to change directions and run back to His loving care.

Lord,

Your will is often inconvenient and narrow, but You ask us to get aligned with it simply because You want us to be part of something truly worthwhile. Help us grab on tightly with both arms to whatever You have for us, knowing it has Your hand on it.

In Jesus' Name, Amen.

TAKE A STAND

Proverbs 28:1

I've always been an introvert, but I still try to put myself out there and be outgoing as much as I feel able. Because this doesn't come naturally to me, I often just try to stay in my lane or avoid rocking the boat. In this "sweet" spot, I'm not standing out or isolating myself. It's "just right" without fear of being mauled by bears. Feeling like this is common as believers, especially in college, where we opt to stay silent when the "opinion committee" that is the campus population finds its mic in *your* face about what you believe about a particular topic with stones at the ready. There is such a thing as being *too* salty, and we don't want to be known as just a loud voice where there are already so many of those. That being said, when God gives us a platform—whatever that looks like—to live and speak boldly like Jesus, I know I'm guilty of trying to find a way out because doing that is plain uncomfortable a lot of times. It's hard to offer a perspective on something that would earn you the label of "bigot" by the world. It's also not easy to offer to pray for an unbeliever because you might get another hurtful label as "religious zealot." It's particularly hard to be honest about your struggles so someone else feels understood as they are sharing theirs. Thanks to the resurrection, we don't have to hide in the shadows but be open about God and people as we were always supposed to be before the Fall. Greater love of Jesus leads to greater love of people that leads to more truth-telling, inevitably leading to boldness becoming a habit. Bold people have nothing to hide, so we should be diligent in making sure we live in a way where that is the case. Let us boldly obey God and leave the consequences to Him.

God,

Thank You for giving us a tongue to speak words that point others to You in the contexts we have been able to and are invited to do. Give us the boldness to speak life and truth in a world of darkness and lies.

In Jesus' Name, Amen.

DON'T BUDGE

1 Corinthians 15:58

In Sam Elliot's song "Won't Back Down"[35] (legends prefer his rendition over Tom Petty's any day), he boasts he could be stood up against the gates of hell, and *even then*, he wouldn't back down. That's good for Sam Elliot, but not everyone has a deep Southern drawl or a mustache that would send shivers up the Enemy's spine. The thought of the devil having our picture on a dart board can lead me to believe this whole "following Jesus" thing is more trouble than it's worth. We're in a spiritual world, and that means we are the target of the spiritual enemy. He knows the power of standing firm in Christ and how big of a detriment it is to his plans. Like any other predator, he's not going to go after the big strong adult that is our Heavenly Father but His weak and vulnerable offspring: us. He would love nothing more than to get a few more passengers on his sinking ship by getting us to compromise our integrity or God's Word. Even if we strive to be immovable in our obe-

---

35 Sam Elliott, "Won't Back Down," *Spotify*, https://open.spotify.com/track/3YopnUHNatnlOj2YMcgGAL.

dience, we can still fear as though it doesn't matter and all the sacrifices we make for Him don't amount to much. This is especially true if we consistently obey but nothing seems to really change. Why *else* would he try to lead us astray? Even if you don't see the benefits now, don't cave in to the pressure, but stay true to who God is and who He created you to be. In time, you'll find that joy and obedience are one and the same.

God,

So many times we bang our heads against the walls thinking sticking close to Your will is all for nothing. Help us see that You are cheering for us in this fight to stay faithful and that when we stand for You, we're standing with You right beside us holding our hand.

In Jesus' Name, Amen.

DAY 80

HEART-DESIRE DOESN'T EQUATE TO HIS DESIRE

Jeremiah 17:9

Something our culture tells us over and over and over again is to follow your heart. We've become a "what's good for you and what's good for me" society, not wanting to stand in the way of getting one's desires out of fear of being labelled "controlling." We can find God's standards and His truth too "oppressive" and decide we're a better master and compass of our lives than He would be. Here's the thing, though: *realistically*, if we said "yes" to *every* whim and desire we had, we'd be dead by the end of the month. If we treat *every* desire we have as a good cause, how do we know what's right or wrong? Furthermore, where would the accountability be if nothing's off the table? Jesus is very attractive to a lot of people, but when His command to die to ourselves and submit to Him daily is naturally brought up, they back out, deciding giving up their own way is very inconvenient for them. I know when I don't "feel" God's presence, I can cling to my ever-changing and subjective feelings more than His unchanging and true Word. We can "feel" as though something is God's will for us, knowing full well it violates His Word, not that we would know if we haven't opened it up for a while. People have the false assumption that following our hearts is good, natural, and freeing when in reality, it continues to keep us in slavery. Think about it: if our hearts were good on their own, would Jesus have had to go to the tremendous lengths He did to change them? If He removed our hearts and their ability to want things, we would be apathetic robots. So Jesus isn't taking away our hearts but changing them along with our will, drive, and desires to match His as Ezekiel promised He would (Ezekiel 36:26-27). It's true that filtering our desires through His Word and doing life on His terms can be quite painful. It's also true that there is no other way to experience such freedom and joy. Additionally, when we lose ourselves to Him, we find ourselves becoming our true self with our true desires because we find them in Him.

Jesus,

Apart from the Holy Spirit and Your resurrection, there is no regeneration in us and nothing good and pure that can be maintained. Give us restraint and trust that when You tell us "no," what You're really doing is giving us what our hearts really need: You.

In Jesus' Name, Amen.

SIMPLIFICATION

Hosea 6:6

After several centuries or so of being oppressed by the Romans, it's probable the average Jew got his or her hopes up that their generation would be the one to witness the Messiah. He would surely be their rescue from the taxation and foreign invaders; in the meantime, they would have to make the best out of it and wait for Him to arrive. The Pharisees, having the best intentions, opted to use that time to be useful, devoting themselves to prayer, studying the scriptures, and giving out of their own pocket. If any Jew was going to be caught with their hand in the cookie jar when the promised Savior arrived, it wasn't going to be them. It was to their surprise that when the Jewish Messiah finally came, He pointed out that they broke the jar a long time ago and their religiosity came down to exactly bupkis, meaning nothing at all. What's more, He wasn't associating with them, who supposedly gave more credence to God's law than most, but the outcasts who had been rightly shunned in some cases and gave no credence to the Word. I hate feeling useless and want to make the most of what

God has given me. That, however, can lead to me feeling as if I'm more worthy of a "gold star" than another person. Jesus showed them and us that true spirituality isn't looking spiritual but *being* spiritual in the way we radically love others. If you want to be useful for the Kingdom, stop trying to be useful and just focus on making Christ your number one and giving His love away like candy.

Lord,

Thank You for calling us deeper to you—but remind us that it's never at the cost of genuine intimacy or love for others. Please humble us to see where all equal targets of Your boundless grace are and stop trying to earn what Christ already accomplished.

In Jesus' Name, Amen.

TAKE MY ADVICE

Proverbs 15:22

I'm willing to bet that out of everyone in the whole world, I'm the worst when it comes to taking advice or accepting criticism. I know my parents love me and want me to succeed when they offer me feedback, but my pride makes their loving correction seem like a personal attack. When we make decisions based on God's Word and discernment from Him, we have a solid foundation. That being said, it's amazingly helpful to get an outsider's take and see their perspective on a situation you might never have considered had you not asked. I cannot tell you how many times I got someone's take on something, and my eyes got real wide after they gave me their take. I'm then like, "OOOOH, that actually makes sense." We shouldn't blindly accept everyone's advice. We have to filter it through Scripture and the Spirit's help, but to not take advice because we think we're *that* good is foolish. I know because I've done that so many times. My dad always says he wishes people didn't have to learn from failure but still accept their fallen state. We can make the assumption that the people trying to advise us don't understand the fear of making mistakes at this critical time in our lives. That's the thing, though: they *do*. Often, they get their wisdom after failing and are trying to save us the headache of going through a mistake to obtain wisdom when we could just have it at our fingertips. Let's not do the stupid thing of trying to figure it all out ourselves and appreciate those who care for our spiritual well-being enough to point out areas of improvement.

Father,

Your discipline only stems from one place, and that's Your steadfast love. Give us hearts that are willing to be instructed and lead us into greater truth that is not possible otherwise.

In Jesus' Name, Amen.

HOW MUCH DO YOU WANT?

Revelation 3:15-16

In the story, *Goldilocks and the Three Bears,* an innocent bear family finds their house invaded by a young, blonde intruder. She has the nerve to go through their house and sit in their chairs, sleep in their beds, and, *gasp,* eat their porridge! The little monster gets away totally off the hook for her home invasion, but that's probably not what you immediately think when considering that parable. When she appropriates the bear's porridge, she notes one cup is too hot while another is too cold. When she finds one in the middle, she approves, as it's "just right."

I'm guilty at times of wanting God but only to the extent to which I can maintain my comfort. I don't want to ignore Him, but at the same time, I don't want to make Him my absolute everything. I can treat this relationship with Him like a class where I don't want to fail but am only willing to do the bare minimum to pass. Jesus spitting us out of

His mouth is terrifying; the sentence "I never knew you" is more so (Matthew 7:21-23). This salvation isn't one of the many things we have going on in our life; it truly is everything. Jesus lets us choose, though, how closely we'll walk with Him, and it's stated later in the chapter that, like any gentleman, He knocks at the door waiting for our response. I think we all want to say "Yes" to living sold out for Jesus but hesitate due to the challenge of letting go of things that make us comfortable. Believe me, I've been there, and it's still hard to go all-in every day. God's been speaking to me that unless I make hard changes in my life, I'll miss out on the life He promised to those who fear Him. I want to hear the words, "Well done, My good and faithful servant" more than anything else that might reach my ears at the end of my life. I implore you to make your life count for Christ and keep seeking Him.

Lord,

May we not go through life doing the bare minimum in our service of You. Give us the boldness and endurance to see what really living for You looks like and how it could change everything.

In Jesus' Name, Amen.

NOT BEING FINE IS FINE

Psalm 62:8

"It's fine. No, **really**, it's no big deal. I—I'm good. Honestly."
Cue eye twitch Ok, maybe I haven't done the latter as
much, but in the past, I've indulged in the former when
someone asks me how I'm doing and I decide to exagger-
ate so they don't worry. I can't even fathom the amount of
times I've "performed" like that in front of God. One reason
I don't tell Him about the doubts and frustrations I have is
that a lot of them are accusations pointed in His direction.
I don't want to be ungrateful for all the amazing things He's
done for me or make Him seem anything less than perfect and exalted in my mind. We have a lot of responsibility representing Christ, but I can put so much unnecessary
pressure on myself trying to act like following God means
you always have it all together. The truth is, admitting your
utter reliance on God is a great witness to the refuge David
states in this psalm. We're not fooling God for one second
when we praise Him, whatever our intention, and curse
Him in our hearts: we're just acting like His enemies as David describes in verse four of this psalm. If you harbor a

curse against God or think He's not doing what He should, just tell Him. He wants to hear it. Not because you're right, but breakthrough happens in our trust of God when we stop acting and start getting real. We need to be cautious about airing our grievances to Him and make sure it's a safe space between us and God without spiritual interference from you-know-who. Satan can easily put a piece of metal in the vacuum of our minds if we give our curse without preparing our minds to hear from God. God doesn't like everything in our hearts, but He still wants to hear about it. It doesn't have to be pretty. He can handle whatever turmoil is in you. He proved that on the cross.

Holy Spirit,

You see so clearly the things that weigh us down and weigh heavily on our hearts. Help us give them to You without feeling like we have to edit them to make them pretty. Help us get the honesty part of this relationship right and start being truthful about how we're doing.

In Jesus' Name, Amen.

ALL WE GOT
AND ALL WE NEED

Ephesians 2:10

In *Wreck-It Ralph*,[36] the titular nine-foot-tall arcade "bad guy" gets tired that his lot in life is being thrown off a building by Nice-landers who dislike him even when the game isn't being played. Even the cordial and friendly playable hero of the game Fix-it Felix is uncomfortable around him, and Ralph has to live isolated while still being able to see Felix being showered with friends, pie, and literal gold medals. Against the advice of other arcade villains who have come to peace with their role, he goes "Turbo," the video game version of AWOL, and goes to another game to win a gold medal and to finally gain the acceptance and friends he's wanted for thirty years. Eventually, he gets the medal he always wanted at the small price of his game almost being shut down, another game being ruled with a saffron fist in King Candy, and a friendship broken with Vanellope von

---

36 *Wreck-It Ralph*. Directed by Rich Moore, performances by John C. Reilly, Sarah Silverman, Jack McBrayer, and Jane Lynch, Walt Disney Animation Studios, 2012.

Shweetz, a fellow outcast. Thankfully, he set things right for his and Vanellope's games. He realizes two important things: that he's bad and that's good—and that he'll never be good and that's not bad.

We can be frustrated at what God's called us to be and do, complaining it's not that notable or exceptional. I remember one time when someone read my palm (which is not biblical at all and would *not* recommend it) and said I would lead a good but unextraordinary life. I have forgiven her since for saying that, but I felt a part of my innocence die and was convinced that I wouldn't amount to much. It's amazing that we are chosen by God and called to things He prepared long in advance for us, and just how much *better* His direction is than what we plan. Our role in life is blessed and handpicked by God. That's the very definition of exceptional in a world that wants exclusive rights and claims to what the word means. Your part is not more or less important, but that doesn't change the fact that how you further the Kingdom is *very* important in God's eyes.

God,

When You look at us, You don't see what the world sees or even what we see in ourselves. You see the man or the woman that was created for amazing things and an essential part of Your plan to show pieces of Heaven on Earth.

In Jesus' Name, Amen.

TAKING CARE OF THE ENGINE

1 Corinthians 10:7

You may have heard the "Freshman 15" myth where students coming into college gain that number of pounds with the student meal plan at their fingertips. It may not be fifteen pounds exactly, but we can pick up the bad habit of being empty pits and spend more time thinking about food than we probably should. Please don't think I'm coming down on you. Really, I get it. If you were to ask my mom how to find me if I got lost in the woods, she would recommend you follow the quinoa, salmon, and Greek yogurt trail that goes on for a few miles. We're still in the last few years of developing physically and can afford to eat more than people in the later stages of life. Furthermore, there may be things about your health you have to consider, and spiritual disciplines like fasting from food may not be safe for you depending on your body's needs. Like other things God gave us, food isn't bad. I think we can all agree that good food is good. It invites you to literally taste the creativity of God, and there are few things I enjoy more than having meaningful conversations over a shared meal. However, like so many other good things we were created to enjoy, we can worship it over our Creator. Even healthy meals can be idolized and treated as something they're not, which is something I've struggled with in the past. We are a consuming culture that can't seem to ever get enough because we think that whatever ready-made meal will satisfy the deeper longing in our hearts for joy, contentment, and peace. Jesus promised us in the book of John that He is the bread of life, and we will never hunger or thirst if we have Him (John 6:35). The next time you have a bountiful harvest in front of you, enjoy it, knowing you're already feasting on that bread and seeking to develop the hunger more and more.

Jesus,

Thank You for the creativity in what we physically consume and digest. May we not take it out of its proper place and cease to worship You in our feasting.

In Jesus' Name, Amen.

TOTAL REDEMPTION

John 13:34-35

Rosaria Butterfield was a lesbian English professor specializing in queer theory at Syracuse University. She was aware of how she was viewed by the average Christian at the time and wrote an article criticizing the church. The hate mail piled and piled up with one notable exception. The author of the letter was a pastor named Ken. He wrote in a kind and empathetic tone. He wanted to engage and understand Butterfield rather than treat her as the "other" despite their disagreements on sex and relationships. The pastor and his wife eventually invited Butterfield over to have dinner: it all surprised her greatly. Before the dinner, the couple humbly and contritely prayed about their sin in a way that caught the English professor totally off guard. They talked with her and seemed to genuinely enjoy her company, without so much as mentioning the gospel or inviting her to church once during their first meeting. She was delighted that they saw her as a person and a friend, not a project. It was this hospitality that led her to start reading the Bible, and she eventually repented and gave her life to Christ, seeing a tiny glimmer of the depths of His love through this couple.[37] If I'm being honest, I can treat the non-Christians in my life as projects. I do my best to be loving and kind while hoping it can lead to conversations about Jesus. We should always strive to be intentional but if we see a person as a quota, they're going to rightfully feel insulted and feel unloved. Putting in a good word for Jesus is great, but there might not always be enough time to fully state the gospel message in every encounter with someone. What we always have time for is to show others the love of God in a real and practical way that will draw them to Jesus. Let's strive to remember that as Christians, we shouldn't see others as part of an objective to complete. We should see them as real people who need God's love.

Lord,

We've been welcomed into Your family and desire for others to become our brothers and sisters in Christ. May we never lose mutuality in our relationships and see each person as unique and valuable and not just a box to check.

In Jesus' Name, Amen.

---

37 Rosaria Butterfield, *The Gospel Comes with a House Key: Practicing Radical Ordinary Hospitality in Our Post-Christian World* (Crossway, 2018).

MINISTRY OF INTERRUPT-ABILITY

Mark 5:21-43

No one likes to be known as a "busy" person. The negative connotations associated with that such as being a stick in the mud or the vibe as though you're oh-so-important. Jesus certainly had His plate full, to say the least, but still made time to make minor pit stops when He had to. In this story, a teacher of the law puts aside the typical puffing-up associated with his position and comes to Jesus as a scared father on behalf of his dying daughter. Jesus, of course, agrees to heal her. However, they are initially delayed by the crowd around Him desiring to see the Teacher they've all heard about. Amidst the masses is a woman who has been afflicted with severe bleeding for many years. She touches Him and instantly gets healed from her condition. Jesus felt His power come out of Him and reasoned *someone* got healed by His power. Knowing whoever they were was in far better condition after touching His robe, Jesus could have just continued on His way. That wasn't going to cut it for Him, though. He stopped His planned route temporarily to find the person who reached out to Him. He sees the woman. He listens to her story. He calls her "*Daughter*," something she didn't think she was to anyone anymore. He didn't forget to heal the Pharisee's daughter as was His original goal, but He wasn't in such a rush as to miss the opportunity to encourage this woman and adopt her into His Kingdom. When we're tempted just to do our own thing in this season of our lives, we should instead aspire to be known as diligent in what God asks us to do but also interruptible so we don't miss out on how His love can be poured onto others through us. We will still have our obligations to do from here on out, but thankfully, He always gives us time in our day to make someone else's.

Abba,

Forgive us for putting faithfulness on our timetable rather than submitting the margins of our day to You. Help us slow down and see the invitations You constantly send out to us throughout the day.

In Jesus' Name, Amen.

LIFE = A BOX OF CHOCOLATES

Numbers 6:24-26

In *Forrest Gump*,[38] the hapless Alabama-born title character native enlists in the Army under Lieutenant Dan Taylor's command. Lieutenant Dan is under no illusions about what he thought God's plan for his life was: to die an honorable death in war serving his country, just like every generation of his family before him. Things, however, don't go his way when nearly all of his squadron is killed in an enemy ambush, and his legs are damaged so badly they have to be amputated. Thankfully, Forrest saves his life, but Lieutenant Dan doesn't see it as a new chance but rather destiny denied as he was not granted a warrior's death with his men. Instead, he has to go on in life as a "legless freak," in his words, and is not only bitter at Gump for saving him but God, thinking he was robbed of something noble. He starts to spiral down into drugs and empty relationships along with dealing with PTSD, revealing it was never fate he was

38 *Forrest Gump*, directed by Robert Zemeckis, performances by Tom Hanks, Gary Sinise, Robin Wright, and Sally Field (Paramount Pictures, 1994).

robbed of but peace. Forrest, when starting his shrimping business in honor of his friend Bubba, kindly and innocently enlists Lieutenant Dan as his first mate, who promised half-sarcastically that he would assume that role should Gump ever become a captain. After a storm tosses their boat around for a bit, it ceases with the added benefit of drawing out all the shrimp the other ships missed out on. Lieutenant Dan finally gets clarity and thanks Gump for saving his life in that dark jungle. In Forrest's words, "He never actually said so, but I think he made his peace with God."

Mental health for our generation is not in a good place overall, and we can do all sorts of things to find some semblance of peace only to be left feeling emptier than we were before. I know I've watched and put things in front of my eyes and mind I shouldn't have, trying to feel peace on my own terms before Jesus stepped in. I can confidently say that although there are some things to work out still, I've never known a greater joy or peace knowing He brought peace between me and God as Paul says in Romans 5. Whatever healing or peace you think you're exempt from because of what you did or what happened to you, know He's looking at you with the goofiest smile ever and wanting you more than anything else to be restored, not destroyed.

God,

Thank You that You are a God who loves to bring peace to anxious hearts that constantly try to take control of what is not ours to control. Give us Your steadfast peace that's unconditional regardless of the specific circumstances in our lives.

In Jesus' Name, Amen.

HURTS, DOESN'T IT?

Matthew 10:32-33

On one Halloween, I remember being excited to hang out with other kids in my neighborhood close to my age who I thought were my friends. A new older kid had moved into the neighborhood during that time and immediately bonded with them, and I wanted to be "in." Another kid who was younger tagged along with us and was eager to hang out with me in particular, much to my annoyance at the time, as I wanted to disassociate myself from him as he was "keeping me" from my "peeps." In a very lame move on my part, I joined in with the other kids to exclude him by ditching him. *Finally*, I thought. **We** *can finally hang out.* I then got a taste of my own medicine when they talked amongst themselves and treated me as if I were in the background. I felt hurt until I realized I did the exact same thing to someone else only moments earlier. I know I can sometimes be found treating Jesus the same way, where I try to distance myself from Him, worrying how I'll be affected socially. I can shake my head and "tsk, tsk" all day at Peter's denying being associated with Christ thrice when

I'm just as guilty of wanting to maintain my own reputation at the "small" price of selling Christ out. Other believers' zeal and boldness can sometimes be off-putting to me, and I can be embarrassed of *them* who are my brothers and sisters in Christ. Even if I don't deny Him in word and make it clear I identify as a Christian, I can still deny Him by how I live if I continually make it clear I'm not interested in *living* like I'm His child. The world desperately tries to make us hide our light because it knows what a game-changer it is when we embrace God's role in our lives. As believers, we need to pick our battles and read the room about how willing others are to discuss faith matters. We should *never*, though, be ashamed of *who* we are and *whose* we are.

Father,

So often we try to disassociate ourselves from You, fearing what others might think of us. Give us the courage to wear the moniker we carry as Your children with joy and zeal.

In Jesus' Name, Amen.

A WEIRD WAKE-UP CALL

Proverbs 21:4

I recall one time when I was eleven and walking in downtown Fredericksburg during the Christmas season with my folks. The horse carriages are especially popular during the holidays at this time and they ride around with all types of passengers. My young self didn't realize that included green curmudgeons from Whoville who you wouldn't touch with a thirty-nine-and-a-half-foot pole. I kid you not: that December afternoon, I saw the Grinch in all his green gruesomeness on a horse carriage, and I was so shocked I stared long enough for him to take notice from across the street. He looked at me like he wanted to punch me and said, "Don't profile me, bro!" and then carried on as the horse moved forward. I'm pretty sure that was the first time I was ever roasted. Years have passed since then, but that doesn't change the fact that I catch myself still staring at others like they "stink, stank, and stunk." There are some people in my life I just *don't* understand and think they're less than exceptional if they've done things that have hurt me, someone I love, or just anyone. If I'm being honest, while I don't normally talk negatively about someone else, I can still hold contempt for them in my heart and mind. Furthermore, I can pat myself on the back and think I'm doing good at what only the Holy Spirit can do: make a judgment call on someone's heart. To that, God says to me, "Josh, you don't know *jack squat* about so-and-so's heart. It's not your job to determine where their hearts are. It's *mine*." I'm not saying we excuse someone else's bad behavior, but if we were really honest in examining ourselves, you see we're just as unworthy as the person we're accusing. We would do well to examine who we're keeping at a distance with a thirty-nine-and-a-half-foot pole and *why* and let our eyes, hearts, and minds be conformed to how Christ sees others.

Jesus,

So often we try to do only what You can do and look down on others, forgetting that, as it says in Psalm 113, You stoop down to look at us in love and compassion. Help us remove the crud in our eyes and our hearts that makes us view others as something less than Your beloved creations.

In Jesus' Name, Amen.

NUMBING IS GOOD UNTIL IT'S NOT

Ezekiel 36:25-27

My mom, a former dental hygienist of thirty-something years, knows firsthand that putting metal things in someone else's mouth can make them feel a little uncomfortable. That's why if a patient seeks the discomfort to be alleviated slightly, they can ask her to make their gums numb as their teeth's excess plaque is being scraped off. Being numb is helpful for a patient in any type of healthcare work, but it's a big hindrance spiritually as believers. To be numb is to no longer feel conviction from the Holy Spirit in our lives. That can seem slightly appealing at first if I'm being real, but without conviction, the sin in us that would break our hearts is seen as "not a big deal." Without conviction, we won't feel a strong desire to act and get involved in whatever God wants us to do. If we complain about how we don't feel like God is speaking to us, it's quite possible we stopped checking in with Him and made ourselves numb to His gentle whisper. Israel's numbness increased as their idol worship became more and more commonplace and they were too overstimulated on everything but God to see how far they had fallen, much like us. These things we choose to prioritize over Jesus rob us of the first love we initially had for Him, and when He's brought up, He can seem like an annoying obligation rather than *literally everything*. It helps to be vulnerable with the Holy Spirit as you go over your inventory and see what causes you to lose your passion for God and for building His Kingdom. This is a painful process, but God doesn't drown us with guilt or condemnation—as the verse says, He sprinkles us with restoring water and makes us into new people with the Advocate literally living within us (2 Corinthians 5:17).

Lord,

Things You have given us to enjoy such as stories and connections can turn into things that sever our connection from You, like binge-watching or comparison on social media. Give us the grace to make changes and see where we're letting ourselves be deaf to Your gentle whisper.

In Jesus' Name, Amen.

HE'S WON

1 Corinthians 10:13

We've been clothed in Christ's righteousness. Every last cent of our spiritual debt has been paid in full because of Him. Sin is no longer the defining aspect of our lives: He is. Those are amazing truths, but it's also true that we are still capable of being tempted every day and we still do give into the sin we've been redeemed from. We're all tempted in different ways, but I suspect when we look at our past failings, we can notice patterns of sin that most commonly trip us up. When we name and identify specific sins in our lives, we make them less intimidating or ambiguous and see them with the right perspective. For me, I frequently struggle with pride, comparison, and people-pleasing and have verses in my memory stock relating to dealing with those frequent slip-ups of mine. Not having the Holy Spirit to intercede and strengthen us is missing out big time in spiritual warfare, and having other believers to be accountable to is more helpful than I convey here. That being said, trying to pinpoint every sin is a waste of time and energy when the real problem is one of identity. Jamie Winship, in his book *Living Fearless*,[39] made the point that trying to kill every last sin in our hearts and minds without looking at the real source of the problem is like trying to kill all the rats when you could remove the source of garbage attracting them. When we take hold of our identity as a child of God, we'll recognize the depths of His love as He is our Father, and we'll want to avoid sin not out of obligation but because we're committed to making our eternal Father smile. No one has it all together but thankfully He does, so we can draw from His limitless source of strength when we face temptation. It's also incredibly encouraging to know we're fighting *from* a place of victory, not *for* it.

Holy Spirit,

You uniquely call each of us in this war, but it's never by ourselves and never without the knowledge that Jesus went through the daily grind of resisting the Enemy like we do. Show us that You're not a disappointed sergeant but a loving Father who cheers for even the smallest victory against sin in our life.

In Jesus' Name, Amen.

---

39 Jamie Winship, *Living Fearless: Exchanging the Lies of the World for the Liberating Truth of God* (Revell, 2022).

COOLER HEADS, SOFTER HEARTS

Ephesians 4:27

My best friend Chris and I joke that when people ask, "What would Jesus do?" when they're in a situation, they'll more often than not want to flip tables and kick everyone's butt if it's a Monday. After seeing people utterly disrespect His Father and His house, rather than have Heaven conjure a whip, Jesus made a whip, was absolutely simmering the whole time He made it, and then promptly gave those people a premature exit, Indiana Jones style. It's a reminder that our Lord is not soft about blatant and unrepentant sin and gets angry like us at injustice. The thing is, though, unlike us, every single time He got angry on Earth, He never took it overboard or allowed His frustration to take the driver's seat. He taught the disciples to turn the other cheek while demonstrating the "when" and "how" of godly anger. Our anger is, by nature, selfish, where we only take into account how *we've* been wronged or how we *"deserve"* to be treated better than we were. As we're becoming more and more like Jesus, the goal is that hopefully, we can deal with difficult people or situations in a way that doesn't bottle our anger but doesn't go anywhere without a leash, ideally held by God. It's helpful to know what triggers your anger and keep the operator's line on with God in prayer when your blood's boiling. Taking a deep breath is commonly recommended because, the thing is, it *works*. If possible, going on a walk in His creation and talking it out with Him can really help give you some perspective on what is really irritating you. And no one will ever get far in dealing with this workable area or any area, for that matter, without regular consumption of God's Word, intentional community, or strength by the Holy Spirit. It's also important once you cool down to own up and apologize for any mistake *you* made in whatever was getting you worked up. This is an area I'm still working on, to be completely honest. It does get easier when I remind myself that God poured out His full anger on sin—I wasn't the target. With that knowledge, I can cope with the person who continually gets under my skin for probably the same reason I'm getting under theirs.

God,

You never cease to be just, otherwise there would have been no need for the cross. In Your anger though, You never cease to be merciful even though we're wholly undeserving of it. May we see You allow us to express our anger, but may we do it in a way that honors and glorifies You.

In Jesus' Name, Amen.

DEPENDENCY CAN HURT

Isaiah 33:6

Before he was the corporate tycoon and adventurer ex-
traordinaire that he is today, Scrooge McDuck was a wee
lad from Scotland who was born into a family barely above
the poverty line. After working his tail feathers off, he got
stiffed and vowed he would never be conned again or do
the conning. He vowed he would make his fortune by being
tougher than the toughies and smarter than the smarties
and make it all square.[40]

We're told over and over again that if we have the right
strength, smarts, and integrity, then we can build a meaningful life we can be proud of. I think we all want our life to
count for *something* bigger than ourselves, and, as young
adults but even more so as followers of Jesus, we want to
pull our weight and take responsibility for our lives. We
desperately want to keep it together because we don't

---

40 Carl Barks, "The Last of the Clan McDuck," *The Life and Times of
Scrooge McDuck* (Gladstone Publishing, Apr. 1994).

want to dishonor God and we recognize how we live our lives deeply affects our witness to the gospel for better or for worse. In the process of this, it can be very easy to put all the pressure and burdens of keeping all your ducks in a row on yourself. I'm guilty of sometimes saying to God in my motives, "Take a load off, Lord. I'm good doing it on my own." I'm thankful He's honest and gracious enough to say, "No, Josh. You *can't* do it on your own. If you could, there would be no point in sending My Son on everyone's behalf." Trying to hold together everything in our lives by our own strength is not only exhausting but a sign of pride stepping in because we're basically telling God we play His role better than He can. We're still to be active participants in how He moves, but the secret to a meaningful life is knowing who God is first and foremost—the strongest foundation possible.

Lord,

We're not capable on our own merits to lead the life we want to live or be the people we want to become. It all rests on a relationship with You, Lord, to go where You go and do the things Jesus did on Your strength, not our own.

In Jesus' Name, Amen.

THE ONE AND ONLY

John 14:6

Moral relativism is a very popular idea nowadays, especially in our age demographic. It's basically the idea that everyone has their own truth and it is completely their prerogative to live their "truth," as if the truth is moldable to whatever is most convenient to their lifestyle. It treats the notion that there is objective truth irrespective of personal opinion as rubbish and that any attempt to say something is objectively right or wrong is oppressive nonsense. When someone claims that there is no absolute truth, I'm thinking, "Huh. That sounds an awful lot like an objective truth claim." I would then ask that person if it's *true* that there is no truth, which would hopefully get their gears turning about the innate self-defeating nature of living by subjective truth. Apologist Frank Turek makes a spot-on observation that between feeling happy and the truth, most people are going to gravitate toward the former even if it's in direct opposition to reality.[41] We have so many options in our

---

41 Frank Turek, *I Don't Have Enough Faith to Be an Atheist* (Crossway, 2004).

culture of what to consume, whom to hang out with, and how to do things that we can treat Him as just as commonplace and unique as other options. Jesus, however, didn't budge—and still doesn't—about His claim to be the one and only way to a right relationship with God. His sacrifice on the cross is the only thing that can completely wash our slate clean and redeem us. People can admire the depths of His love until they realize that His resurrection means He has the authority to say what is wrong in our lives and that's a price too costly for a lot of people. That being said, truth should trump personal feelings every time, and while it's still hard to walk this narrow road, it's worth it because it's true and ultimately where the joy is.

Jesus,

Your claims about Yourself have a tendency to be seen as exclusive in today's culture because they are. No one can come to You and receive You without losing themselves and what they define as true. Whatever we give up for You is never in vain as we get to walk in the way, live in the truth, and experience life as it was meant to be lived.

In Your Name, Amen.

PART OF THE CLUB

1 Samuel 2:8

At Riverbend High School, there was a time between classes called "Bear Block" named after our mascot, that was
reserved for study hall or clubs and such. I volunteered
with the Friendship Club, a club that helped students with
disabilities find connection and encouragement between
their classes. We did a collab cake party with the Finance
Club, and it went pretty well. I stayed to help clean with the
Finance Club before they headed to the auditorium to take
their group photo for the yearbook. I was about to head out
when the club sponsor, Ms. Fethrens, called my name and
told me to come with them to take the picture. Confused,
I tried to decline and explain I wasn't *part* of the Finance
Club. Smiling, she replied, "Trust me. You're in." I decided
to go along with it and head to the auditorium and was
among those pictured for the Finance Club despite not being a member. My parents encouraged me to just take the
win, but I didn't want to presume I was part of something
I wasn't a part of. I kind of felt like an imposter. I can still
feel like that at times if I'm being honest. Like this life He's

inviting me to live and the blessings that go along with are for someone else, not me. I don't have childlike faith and go forward in bold confidence; I tend to overanalyze everything and remain stationary. I'm not as kind as I think I am; I'm very prone to be selfish and not consider how others might be doing. I'm not always good at obeying when it's hard; I have a toxic relationship with comfort zones at times. Along with all the blessings He's given me, I can feel like a total stranger at His table, despite Him being the perfect Host and Guest. What on *earth* did I do to deserve any of it? The answer: I didn't. Neither did you. God chose us because He's that good and He doesn't want us to miss out on knowing we *do* belong and *do* have a seat waiting for us at His table. Instead of coming up with all the reasons why you *don't* belong, just take God on His Word that you do and bank that when He tells you in the vein of a cool financial teacher, "You're in," you're *in*.

Father,

We praise You for Your heart that can't help but welcome in us from the slums, streets, and pits of our own making. Give us grace to see that our standing before Heaven is secure and steady because it has Your hand on it.

In Jesus' Name, Amen.

MEME MOTIVATION

James 1:22-25

"DO IT! JUST DO IT!" is an exhortation of Shia LeBeouf from a YouTube video back in 2015.[42] Viewers on the Internet noted the video's inherent hilarity and motivation that they can just do "it," whatever "it" is, and that nothing can stop them from doing "it." When I feel a calling from God, rather than just step forward in faith and do what He asks, I can spend my time overthinking it to death wondering if it's *really* from God or just my imagination. Sometimes I do this because my natural default state is to overthink. There are also other times I subconsciously do this because I'm hoping someone *else* will do it. Spending time meditating on God's Word and its meaning is so crucial, but that's not the only part of it. We're to act on it daily and examine our lives and see what areas need conforming to it. I'll be honest: part of the reason I don't obey as boldly as I should sometimes is because I doubt God's Word as a trustworthy

---

42 Shia LaBeouf, "Shia LaBeouf 'Just Do It' Motivational Speech (Original Video by LaBeouf, Rönkkö, & Turner)," *YouTube*, uploaded by MotivaShian, 31 Aug. 2015, https://www.youtube.com/watch?v=ZXsQAXx_ao0.

foundation. That doubt comes from not believing that God Himself is a trustworthy foundation. I'm really afraid of being let down and while I recognize His Word is always reliable, I'm afraid of what will happen if I really strive to obey what the Bible says wholeheartedly. I'm afraid of losing what is known, safe, and comfortable. I'm afraid of losing myself. It's still a work in progress but what I've been trying to do recently is ask myself every few minutes, "How can I obey God's Word?" and then I do whatever that means in that particular moment. We can't do what we don't know, so before we even think about going forward in action, we have to get engaged with the Word all the time. It's scary to take God's word on His Word, but let's strive to do the next right thing.

God,

You trust us to do great things; that's heavy, Father. So often we see it as yet another obligation of our busy lives and fail to see it for the grand and wonderful invitation it really is. Show us ways to keep staying connected to You and not hesitate to know You're with us every step of the way.

In Jesus' Name, Amen.

PLEASING GOD, NOT MAN

Galatians 1:10

Some people have never touched alcohol in their lives, but everyone probably needs some accountability in the form of a recovery group. If not for drinking, I guarantee it'll be for *something* else. For me, if I were to go to a specific recovery group, I would start off with "Hello, my name is Josh, and I'm a people-pleaser," and they'll reply with a supportive "Hi Josh." I'm proud to say I've been sober from that for about ... eight hours if I'm leveling with you. There's a good chance I could slip soon if the prospect of someone liking me just a *little* bit more if I do something for them presents itself." That's not to say serving others is a bad thing: quite the opposite, as Jesus expects that to be regular and commonplace as His disciples. People-pleasing, in my experience, is rarely done to honor Christ and put the interests of others above my own as Paul says in Philippians 2. It's done so we can find our worth and identity as we're being affirmed what a good boy or good gal we are. Few things make me more anxious than the thought of letting some- one down or disappointing them in any way. That just goes back to the inherent selfishness in people-pleasing where *we* are still the focus and are really using others' times of need to make ourselves feel better. Saying "No" is also a struggle for struggling people-pleasers because we never want to deny an opportunity to greatly impact the King- dom. What I've learned the hard way is that if I say "Yes" to everything, I'm saying "Yes" to nothing really and leaving myself more drained than I was before. Hear this: saying "No" is okay if you really can't do it. I'm not saying you make it a habit but not only is it okay to say it when you need it, it's biblical. We're never going to please everyone all the time. It's inefficient to try to do so. Therefore, a more pro- ductive use of our energy and time is to please *God* in all we do, which has infinitely better returns physically, mentally, and spiritually than the former.

God,

We're created to serve You and others, exclusively in that or- der. Forgive us for the times where others are unloved by us in our attempts to find validation in them rather than in You. Help us know it's okay to go against what everyone else is doing if it makes You pleased.

In Jesus' Name, Amen.

THE GREATEST CHALLENGE AND JOY

Psalm 105:4

I *do* love Jesus. All the time, every day. I don't always *like* following Him, though. Being saved is amazing beyond words, but it's *not* a trivial matter. It changes *everything*. This thing called a relationship we have with God should now be the center of our lives from which every thought, word, and action stems. At first glance, that seems like an immense burden, and I don't always see it as the true life it is. We can do the things associated with abiding in God like praying, reading the Word, godly community, and other things because we feel, well, *stuck* with Christ, rather than out of love. I know I can be resigned and know lukewarmness isn't an option so I commit to seeking Him out daily but with gnashed teeth and a hardened heart all the while, thinking I'm getting cheated out of something "better." At times, I wish I could escape the responsibilities thrust upon me as an ever-growing disciple of Christ. At my lowest times, I wished this whole thing was a con so I could just dip and leave at my convenience. We can mistake the idea that some space between us and God is good, failing to realize that only applies to fallible, finite human relationships. The lie the Enemy often whispers is that we're missing out when we give our lives to Jesus. That, somehow, we're losing everything for nothing. That's partly true. We *are* losing everything, but it's *not* for nothing. We were created *for* God with the intent that the intimacy of our relationship with Him would grow ever deeper. Being an active participant and drawing near to Him is hard, and like every relationship, it takes work, but in my experience, literally *nothing* encapsulates life more than that. If you find yourself "not feeling like it," just imagine what you would do for God if you *did* feel like it, then do that. Usually, the feelings will catch up with you. God is currently working on my heart to prefer Him over feeling good. *Believe* me, I'm still struggling to make Him my center, and just to clue you in case you didn't know, true discipleship is rarely an easy thing. I promise you, though; it's so worth it.

Jesus,

Nothing produces more joy, love, and freedom than when we do life pursuing You wholeheartedly. Thanks for the opportunities You give us daily to go deeper in Your love and Presence. Help us take advantage of this lifeline we call a relationship with You and see where it takes us for the rest of our lives.

In Jesus' Name, Amen.

CLOSING THOUGHTS

Dang! One hundred days of listening to me rambling on, and you made it. If I ever do write another devotional, I promise I'll dive into more of the interesting nerdy church history stuff along with more moderated pop-culture references as much as is possible for me. Seriously, though, if you take anything away from this book, it's to not put your faith on a trophy shelf that rusts away. Continue working it out and let it affect more and more areas of your life. I don't want to think that just because I wrote this, that means I'm somehow more spiritual than I am. Spoiler alert: I'm not. I'm a ragamuffin who God decided was worth sending His Son to die for. I'm an active work in progress that takes a while because I *am* a piece of work. What I'm invited to do is what we're all invited to do. It's the *only* thing we can do: receive and participate. If this book helped you do that in any way, I'm grateful. If not, I take zero offense. Either way, with God's help, I encourage you to keep trucking on faithfully in this life and to the next.